MW01011432

Christmas

IN NEW ORLEANS

Christmas
IN NEW ORLEANS

PEGGY SCOTT LABORDE AND JOHN MAGILL

PELICAN PUBLISHING COMPANY
GRETNA 2009

The word "Pelican" and the depiction of a pelican are trademarks
of Pelican Publishing Company, Inc., and are registered in the
U.S. Patent and Trademark Office.

Library of Congress Cataloging-in-Publication Data

Laborde, Peggy Scott.
  Christmas in New Orleans / Peggy Scott Laborde and John Magill.
    p. cm.
  Includes bibliographical references and index.
    ISBN 978-1-58980-560-6 (hardcover : alk. paper) 1. Christmas—
Louisiana—New Orleans. 2. New Orleans (La.)—Social life and
customs. I. Magill, John. II. Title.
  GT4986.L8L33 2009
   394.266309763—dc22
                                            2009012923

Frontispiece: Kermit Ruffins, playing his trumpet in front of Jackson Square,
welcomes in the 2008 snowfall. (Courtesy the Clarion Herald)

Printed in China
Published by Pelican Publishing Company, Inc.
1000 Burmaster Street, Gretna, Louisiana 70053

Contents

Mayor deLesseps "Chep" Morrison celebrated the City of New Orleans' recent accomplishments, as well as its international ambitions, on his official Christmas card in 1960. (Louisiana Division/City Archives, New Orleans Public Library)

Acknowledgments

The foundation for this book was laid by two programs produced for New Orleans Public Broadcasting Service affiliate WYES-TV: "Creole Christmas" and "Christmas in New Orleans." Thanks to WYES's Beth Arroyo Utterback and Randall Feldman for their continued interest and support of the production of programs that focus on the history and heritage of our city.

Some of the interviews in the book are from those programs. Appreciation goes to Annette Campo, Ashli Richard, and Kelsi Schreiber for transcriptions. Much gratitude to Dominic Massa for his transcription assistance and for his ongoing encouragement. Thanks also go to Ann Masson, whose love of New Orleans' past is a continuing inspiration. Doris Ann Gorman, Sally Kittredge Reeves, Mary Lou Eichhorn, and Betty Bagert have always been available for their very appreciated input. Patricia Brady and John Kemp have always been generous with essential advice.

Special thanks to Priscilla Lawrence, who was responsible for my initial collaboration with John Magill in *Canal Street: New Orleans' Great Wide Way*, also published by Pelican, in 2006. John's extensive knowledge, enthusiasm, and good humor make for a delightful work experience. Also thanks to the Collection for sharing many of the photos that are in this book

Larry Roussarie's assistance and good humor in technical matters pertaining to visual images were most valuable. Friend and photographer George Long helped spread the word in the New Orleans photography community that we were looking for present-day Christmas images.

Pelican Publishing Company's continuing interest in publishing books of a local and regional historical nature is encouraging to those of us eager to contribute and to enjoy reading a body of work in print on our city's rich heritage. Many thanks to Dr. Milburn Calhoun, Kathleen Calhoun Nettleton, Nina Kooij, Scott Campbell, and their fine staff, with whom it remains a continued pleasure to work.

Another treasure trove for New Orleans history research is the New Orleans Public Library's Louisiana Division/City Archives. Irene Wainwright and Wayne Everard were so very supportive. John and I want to thank Libby Bonner for sharing the nineteenth-century journal of Victoria Raymond. These childhood memories added much to our early history section.

Photographers Joe Bergeron, Jan Brantley, Syndey Byrd, Alex Demyan, Brad Edelman, Cheryl Gerber, Del Hall, Coleen Perilloux Landry, Frank Methe, Frank Methe III, Kerri McCaffety, and David Rae Morris have contributed to our book, making it all the more attractive.

And on a more personal note, growing up in a warm and loving family whose parents fostered an interest in New Orleans history has been invaluable in every historical project I've tackled. Thanks to my father and my mother, Warren and Gloria Walther Scott, along with brother Kurt and sister Nancy for many fine Christmas memories. I want to also express gratitude to Uncle Irving and to Aunt June Scott for loving the city so much and instilling in me an appreciation of the city's history.

If ever there were two fans of Christmas, it was Ellis Laborde, my dear father-in-law and for many years manager of City Park, and my friend Martha Hart, a longtime volunteer at WYES. Memories of both, especially during the holidays, make that time all the more special.

Finally, yet foremost, thanks to my husband, Errol Laborde, whose own appreciation of the city's culture, rituals, and celebrations is most inspiring. His wisdom and support make any project I work on all the more possible.

—PEGGY SCOTT LABORDE

Introduction

There are two faces of Christmas, the spiritual feast day of the Nativity of Jesus and the winter celebration, embraced by many cultures. New Orleans, a city with a spiritual legacy but one that also likes to party, embraces the traditional holiday celebration while adding its own embellishments.

Memories of shopping with the family on Canal Street; visiting the decorated homes around town such as the lavish Centanni home on Canal Street or, later, the Copeland home in Metairie; going to see the

Mayor Victor H. Schiro acknowledged the potential that NASA's Michoud plant represented for the city on his 1961 Christmas card. (Louisiana Division/City Archives, New Orleans Public Library)

Today, most of the Christmastime bonfires upriver from New Orleans are designed in a teepee shape. Laura Plantation builds such a fire each year. (Photo courtesy of Laura Plantation Company)

From 1946 through 1966, visiting the Centanni family home on Canal Street was a highlight of the Christmas season. (Courtesy of the family of Myra Centanni Mehrtens)

Ducks in a City Park lagoon didn't seem to mind the rare snowfall of almost four inches that took place on New Year's Eve, 1963. (Photo by Frank H. Methe III, courtesy of the Clarion Herald*)*

bonfires in St. James and St. John Parishes, perched on the Mississippi River levees, the flames brilliant against the black winter sky—all part of Christmas in the New Orleans area. Since Christmas is also very much a musical celebration, caroling in Jackson Square on a December Sunday evening is another of those treasured local traditions.

It can't be a surprise that a city known for its culinary heritage also has a few traditional dishes for the Christmas table. We'll look back at how New Orleanians feasted at this time of the year, even in the most modest and trying of the early days.

For those who have grown up in New Orleans, certainly there is a collective Christmas memory that more often than not contrasts with popular notions of cold weather during the holidays. In a climate that allows for the doors of homes to be thrown wide open, allowing views of the Christmas tree to passersby, a common site is a neighbor wearing tropical garb in the dead of winter. A white Christmas is the stuff of songs and childhood wishes. Of course, there are those rare days of actual snow, and in this book we'll recall some of them.

In New Orleans, post-Christmas letdown simply doesn't exist. Thanks to the initial settlement of the city by French Catholics, today, regardless of faith, you can't escape the fact that on January 6, Twelfth Night marks the traditional end of the Christmas season and the beginning of the Carnival season. Pretty seamless, except that the red and green decorations are suddenly replaced by purple, green, and gold. And fruitcake vanishes to be replaced by king cakes. May you find some "sweet stuff"—shared memories—in the following pages.

—Peggy Scott Laborde

Mr. Bingle, perched above the Canal Street entrance to Maison Blanche at left, reminds shoppers 'tis the season. (Photo by Del Hall)

Christmas
IN NEW ORLEANS

e here with **CHRISTMAS** cheer!

By the time this photograph of Maison Blanche department store was taken by Charles L. Franck Photographers in 1952, the store's Christmas mascot, Mr. Bingle, was as much an icon of the New Orleans Christmas season as Santa Claus himself. (Courtesy of The Historic New Orleans Collection)

CHAPTER ONE

Canal Street at Christmas

If there's one collective memory of Canal Street, New Orleans' historic main thoroughfare, it's of Christmastime. Before America's expansion to the suburbs caused a shift in shopping patterns in most large cities, Canal Street was *the* place in New Orleans to buy Christmas presents and to have your photograph taken with Santa.

There were window displays of luxurious merchandise such as furs and designer evening gowns at Godchaux's, Gus Mayer, and Kreeger's. Decorated window displays were D. H. Holmes' gift to New Orleans. Each year the department store presented a different theme. These windows often depicted wonderlands of imported animated figures that could momentarily transport a window shopper to a Venetian or Dickensian Christmas fantasy, even if the weather outside was a temperate 72 degrees.

Maison Blanche, referred to by locals as "MB," featured Mr. Bingle, a snowman marionette that, from his inception after World War II, did not "melt"even in the subtropics of New Orleans—or under the hot lights of his daily television program during the Christmas season. Although MB has closed, the Dillard's department store chain has continued to feature the snowman. The Mr. Bingle figure that graced the front of MB's lavish facade on Canal Street for many years is today included in City Park's Celebration in the Oaks annual light display. Maison Blanche was once part of the City Stores chain, and other department stores in the group, such as Lowenstein's in Memphis, also adopted the loveable Mr. Bingle as its Christmas mascot.

In addition to the giant Mr. Bingle, a four-story Santa was a downtown fixture for many years. Domenico Marino, who worked for General Outdoor Advertising, designed the St. Nick that greeted shoppers at Sears, on the corner of Baronne and Common Streets. It was a holiday fixture from the early 1940s until 1979. According to Eddie Deubler, who was the Sears building engineer, the Santa was made of plywood and had to be erected in sections: the boots, the legs and round tummy, and finally the smiling face. Santa held a wrapped package labeled, "From Sears."

Most children got to see Santa up close when their parents took them to visit the big fellow at such department stores as D. H. Holmes and Maison Blanche. In the case of the latter, Mr. Bingle also popped up with Santa in many of those photos.

Here Comes Mr. Bingle!

Jingle, jangle, jingle,
here comes Mr. Bingle
With another message
from Kris Kringle,
Time to launch your
Christmas season,
Maison Blanche makes
Christmas pleasin',
Gifts galore for you to see,
Each a gem from MB!

In New Orleans, with its semi-tropical climate, how unlikely is it that a little snowman with an ice-cream-cone hat and holly wings would become a symbol of New Orleans Christmas? His name—Mr. Bingle.

The concept for Bingle came from Emile Alline, Sr., the display director for Maison Blanche department store. On a buying trip to Chicago, Alline discovered that some department stores had their own Christmas mascots. Marshall Field's featured Uncle Mistletoe, a whimsical Santa's helper. Looking as if he sprang from a Dickens novel, this tiny gent sported a sprig of mistletoe on his top hat and a pair of wings on his back. Montgomery Ward department store promoted a holiday character that ultimately became a national treasure: Rudolph the Red-Nosed Reindeer.

Alline pitched the mascot idea to Maison Blanche executives Louis Schwartz and Herbert Schwartz. He called his pint-sized personage a "snowdoll." In an interview in the 1980s, Alline recalled, "I wanted to appeal to kids. I wanted it to be flexible, that we could tie him in with all kinds of displays and so I thought of the ribbon, I thought

Stores on Canal Street were like old friends. Many were locally owned. Even those stores like Woolworth's that were part of national chains employed friendly people who knew their city and their customers, and the stores seemed local even if ownership was not.

From the 1930s through the 1980s, Canal Street was also the setting for occasional Christmas parades. In the early 1960s, miniature renditions of balloon figures resembling those featured in the New York City Macy's Thanksgiving Day Parade floated down the thoroughfare. During Mayor Sidney Barthelemy's administration in the late 1980s, wife Mickey fostered a series of citywide Christmas activities, including a parade.

Crowds watched the parades from the center of Canal Street, on what locals refer to as the neutral ground or median. From the 1930s until 1970 the City of New Orleans employed an official decorator named Betty Finnin. At Christmastime she would transform the historic cast-iron lampposts on the neutral ground into candles or chimneys or adorn them with Christmas wreaths.

Right off Canal, a must-visit during the Christmas season was the Roosevelt Hotel. Its block-long lobby featured a canopy of spun fiberglass known as "angel hair" and almost a thousand ornaments. Not as lavish, but still a special place to visit was the lobby of the St. Charles Hotel, later known as the Sheraton Charles. Strings of colored lights dotted the mezzanine balcony while flocked trees "took root" in the hotel lobby. The hotel was demolished in the 1970s; on the site today is the Place St. Charles office building.

The celebration of the Christmas season on Canal Street changed during the last half of the twentieth century as most retailing shifted to suburban shopping malls. In 1960, Lakeside Mall opened. One of its major stores was a branch of downtown's D. H. Holmes. For a period, it continued its tradition of lavish decorations inside the store, including a wonderland. Over the years, the mall itself has presented annual Christmas displays, including an almost life-size toy train ride for children and a miniature village. While downtown department stores are no more, still remaining in the old Canal Street shopping district are Adler's jewelry store and Rubensteins clothiers. The Shops at Canal Place and the Riverwalk Marketplace are more recent additions to the street. Beyond those recent memories, we have newspapers and memoirs to thank for keeping the more distant past alive.

Canal Street's Early Days

On December 26, 1865, New Orleans' *Daily True Delta* reported, "The Christmas just passed will long be remembered as probably the most demonstrative one witnessed in New Orleans." The streets were thronged with shoppers. Servants carrying market baskets containing Christmas dinner followed many of them. Shops in 1865 opened on Christmas after having stayed open late on Christmas Eve. By midday businesses began to close as people were "visiting place to place, and

This photo from the 1970s shows the bell display that hung above the entrance to D. H. Holmes for many years. The bells tolled in synchronization with Christmas music. (Courtesy of Louis R. Roussel)

Santa greets passersby from his "cottage" above the entrance to D. H. Holmes department store. (Photo by C. F. Weber, courtesy of Bergeron Gallery)

of the ornaments, the leaves and the little mittens of course, just to make it sweet and cute." A contest to name the "snowdoll" was held among employees, and the general manager decided on the winning entry.

Ashleigh Austin, a Mr. Bingle fan who devotes part of her web site to the snowman (ashleighaustin.com), thinks the name may have come from a 1915 novel called *Mr. Bingle.* Written by George Barr McCutcheon, whose most famous tome is *Brewster's Millions,* this is the story of Mr. and Mrs. Thomas S. Bingle, a childless New York couple who provide gifts and a meal to less fortunate little ones on Christmas Eve.

Also fitting in nicely was the fact that Mr. Bingle's initials were "MB," a popular local reference to Maison Blanche.

New Orleans Grammy Award-winning vocalist Irma Thomas remembers Bingle—"I thought he was the cutest little thing. I didn't have a Mr. Bingle doll, but I thought he was kind of cute"—as does local rhythm and blues guitarist/singer/bandleader "Deacon John" Moore. "I do remember Mr. Bingle 'cause my mother used to take us window shopping on Canal Street around Christmas. And Maison Blanche always had a big Mr. Bingle display in the window with Mr. Bingle flying down and then they would make Mr. Bingle talk after a while."

Even before the arrival of Mr. Bingle, plans were underway to present Christmas shows in Maison Blanche's Canal Street store windows. The shows were to include marionettes, wooden figures with strings or wire. Alline found his "Geppetto" just a few blocks away from the store, on racy Bourbon Street.

Edwin "Oscar" Isentrout's Bourbon Street show consisted of marionettes that performed a strip tease, one of many vaudeville-style acts that were sandwiched in between the exotic dancers' performances. Originally from New York, the puppeteer had been traveling around the country with a marionette troupe and, on a whim, decided to buy a bus ticket to New Orleans.

Isentrout initially retained his Bourbon Street nightclub engagement. Since his schedule made it difficult to work for Maison Blanche all day, he sought the help of two talented teenagers, Ray Frederick and Harry J. Ory. The two had achieved some acclaim around town with a marionette act of their own and assisted Isentrout in the early years of the window shows.

According to Ory, "Oscar came in one morning and he was holding a snowman and it had wings. It looked pretty cute. He said, 'Well, Alline wanted us to use the snowman as the star of the show rather than our little blond-headed fellow that we were creating.' We said, 'Maybe it's a good idea.' So we went along with it."

Mr. Bingle made his debut during the 1947 Christmas season. Isentrout and his assistants created a winter wonderland that featured an assortment of characters, but Bingle was center stage. Isentrout became the voice of Mr. Bingle.

Ory adds, "Oscar took that doll and animated it and he gave it character because it was

This nineteenth-century scene from a D. H. Holmes window display included a train called the DHH. (Courtesy of Louis R. Roussel)

imbibing egg-nog. . . . All streets contained living streams of happy 'humans,' merry, joyous and contented; but Canal Street as usual, was the centre of fashion, and all the beauty of the city seemed congregated there." This was the first Christmas after the Civil War. It was in stark contrast to 1861, when the city's economy was in near collapse, right before New Orleans fell to Union forces in April 1862.

By 1865, Canal Street was considered the main street of New Orleans, as it overtook Chartres and Royal Streets as the city's most fashionable shopping district. It had not only evolved into the showcase of upscale trade in New Orleans, but it had become the place where just about everybody in town wanted to congregate during Christmas.

The thoroughfare of Canal Street was born in 1807 as a planned navigation canal connecting the Mississippi River and Lake Pontchartrain. The canal was never built though the name stayed. The street's great width and median are all that are left of the canal plan that appeared on many early maps. By the 1830s, Canal Street, up to its intersection with Royal Street, was a commercial area, but beyond this point it was residential, lined with elegant townhouses. A remaining example of one of these fine houses is the residence built in 1844 for Dr. William Newton Mercer. It still stands as the Boston Club, a private men's club. Beginning in the 1840s, dry goods stores started to invade the residential section of the street and during the next half-century some of those establishments grew into big department stores.

Beginning in the early 1800s, as the Industrial Revolution mass-produced abundant new merchandise, American retailing experienced dramatic changes. Former luxury items became commonplace. The

D. H. Holmes department store's Christmas window decorations were often extravagant. (Courtesy of Louis R. Roussel)

purchase of ready-made clothing, once considered not particularly respectable, became the norm. Newspapers and magazines with mass circulations increased space for advertising. Out of a growing middle class were new consumers eager to buy.

Even if the shops of New Orleans were small and unassuming during the 1830s and 1840s, retailers sold some of the finest merchandise in the United States, befitting the growth and wealth of the city. Stores specialized in very narrow product lines: particular types of fabric, ribbons, hats, or bonnets. The French Quarter showed its French roots in its shops, which were similar to the small eighteenth-century shops of Paris, where merchants more often went to the mansions of their rich patrons than serving the patrons in the shops.

In the 1850s, architect T. K. Wharton, who was the superintendent of construction for the U.S. Custom House, took his children to see the beautifully decorated Christmas windows along Chartres and Royal

his voice. And of course we had a part in that because we designed the mechanical bodies. And you can't have life without movement. So Oscar gave it personality."

For Isentrout, performing Mr. Bingle was much more than a job. Jeff Kent, an apprentice to the puppeteer in the 1980s, recalls the first time he met him. "There was this old, thin, skinny man smoking cigarettes, without filters too. He was a workaholic. All he had was Mr. Bingle. When someone came up to him and started talking to him and if he said, 'Oh, I'm the voice of Mr. Bingle,' then they would just go nuts. It's almost like meeting a star. So that was very important to him."

And much of that popularity can be attributed to the personality that Isentrout gave Bingle. "Mr. Bingle is a child," says Kent. "He is a child that likes to have fun. He gets into mischief. It's usually Mr. Bingle that gets into trouble and Santa Claus usually gets him out of trouble."

The sketches that Isentrout wrote for the window shows turned out to be a big hit. Alline recalls, "People would wait in

Puppeteer Edwin "Oscar" Isentrout gave Maison Blanche's Mr. Bingle a voice and personality. (Courtesy of Jeff Kent)

Oscar Isentrout was hired by Maison Blanche display director Emile Alline, Sr., to create a Mr. Bingle puppet show for the store's Canal Street window. (Courtesy of Jeff Kent)

line and you'd have to walk out in the street, bypassing the sidewalks, to get by. They would wait there just to see the show. We put up rails to keep the people back. We ran ads, almost half-page ads, to say, 'Please stand back and let the little ones see the show too.'"

And literally pulling the strings were Isentrout, Ory, and Frederick. Ory remembers those early years vividly. "We were back there looking down at the marionettes. We had a fan on both sides cooling us off. We got kind of sweaty you know, you would get a little tired doing the same thing over and over and hearing the same record."

In addition to the snowman's appearances in the store's front window, a giant Bingle was mounted above the store's Canal Street entrance.

Alline recalls, "We made a fifty-four-foot Mr. Bingle and put him up on the front of the store. I had to go up to Chicago. They had a manufacturer there; it took two flat cars to get it down from Chicago."

From Thanksgiving to Christmas, the snowman even had his own television show on WDSU-TV. "The kids used to make a

This Venetian scene is a prime example of the effort and expense that went into the window displays at D. H. Holmes at Christmastime. (Courtesy of Louis R. Roussel)

This D. H. Holmes window, depicting an eighteenth-century scene, is an example of the lavish displays that were a Christmas tradition. Louis R. Roussel was in charge of the display department for all of the Holmes stores for many years. (Courtesy of Louis R. Roussel)

This nearly life-size locomotive is an example of the creativity of the display department at D. H. Holmes. (Courtesy of Louis R. Roussel)

Puppeteers Ray Frederick, left, and Harry J. Ory worked with Oscar Isentrout to create the early Mr. Bingle marionette shows that were presented in Maison Blanche's Canal Street window. (Courtesy of Harry J. Ory)

Streets. By Wharton's time fashionable New Orleans shoppers were gravitating a block away to Canal Street, where newer, bigger, better decorated stores were becoming stiff competition.

Manufacturers produced children's toys, dolls, and games in ever increasing quantities, and each holiday season new playthings appeared. By the 1870s there were must-have Christmas items such as Christmas cards, with the holiday further focused on children.

As the main shopping street of one of America's biggest cities, Canal Street was in the midst of this trend. While merchandising expanded and Christmas grew in commercial importance, Canal Street developed into one of the most important shopping streets in the nation. For nearly 150 years it was the Crescent City's best shopping street and the center of the city's secular Christmas celebration.

Canal Street Becomes a Shopping Street

Daniel H. Holmes, a Chartres Street merchant who opened for business in 1842, was among the earliest pioneers to move to Canal Street. In 1849, Holmes, a Kentuckian, opened his new emporium on Canal between Bourbon and Dauphine. Although his contemporaries considered him a madman for moving so far from the heart of the retail district, albeit only a few blocks away, D. H. Holmes' store became an instant success and a pacesetter in New Orleans' growing marketplace.

The store was decorated in the elaborate English Tudor Gothic style, and to enter its rarified halls was like walking into a cathedral of

special effort to watch," Alline says. "It was a little comics along with merchandising, promoting merchandise. At one time our competitive store had Santa Claus on at the same time and the kids would sit on Santa's lap. And he would say, 'What do you want for Christmas?' And this is live television. They'd say, 'A Bingle doll.'"

Bingle even visited children in hospitals. More than a pitchman, Bingle was also a goodwill ambassador.

Other downtown department stores tried to find ways to compete with the popularity of the little snowman. Krauss department store president Hugo Kahn remembers Bingle well. "I was envious of Mr. Bingle. That's not a very nice Christmas thing to be thinking about but I wish we had something like that. And we were always trying to think of what kind of gift we could get that would be like Mr. Bingle. But Mr. Bingle, I think for New Orleans, was real special."

Isentrout died in 1985 and was buried in an unmarked grave in Hebrews Rest #3 Cemetery at the corner of Elysian Fields and

Gentilly Boulevard. Donations and proceeds from a novella called *Saving Mr. Bingle* by Sean Doles were used to construct a grave marker. On it, a sketch of Mr. Bingle is etched into the granite.

The Arkansas-based Dillard's department store chain eventually bought out Maison Blanche and continued producing Bingle items, including dolls and ornaments. Mr. Bingle's initials may not be the same as the store he "represents" but to locals it only matters that he's still around.

This D. H. Holmes window depicts a snowy eighteenth-century forest. (Courtesy of Louis R. Roussel)

This entrance to a Christmas wonderland shows how elaborate the decorations were during the holidays at D. H. Holmes. (Courtesy of Louis R. Roussel)

While visiting New Orleans in December of 1951, Indiana amateur photographer Charles Weever Cushman shot this photograph of downtown Canal Street. (Charles W. Cushman Collection, Indiana University Archives)

merchandising. Holmes' showcase was the elegant Silk Hall, which rose two stories and featured some of the finest fabrics and accessories to be found in the South. It was all designed to make the lady shopper feel rich and to entice her to spend money as if she were.

Dressing up in one's finest to go shopping was *de rigueur* since the shopper was going to see and be seen. During the holiday seasons of the 1870s and 1880s, a visit to D. H. Holmes was like walking into a Christmas card, especially with the store bedecked with garlands and wreaths.

One block from Holmes, between Bourbon and Royal, the Touro block of buildings was built by Judah Touro in the 1850s. This row of fine shops and offices with a common facade was ringed with ornate cast-iron galleries, which were not only fashionable at the time, but protected shoppers from sun and rain. Similar lacy galleries were soon built all along Canal Street's commercial area.

The Touro block was home to some of the Crescent City's finest dry goods, notions, jewelry, silver, and music stores. It had gaslit

As shown in this 1957 photograph, Santa is the main attraction during the Christmas parades that have rolled down Canal Street through the years. (Photo by C. F. Weber, courtesy of Bergeron Gallery)

show windows stretching three hundred feet along Canal Street. At Christmas the windows were adorned with greenery, ribbons, flags, and flowers.

By the 1870s, Canal Street was the center of ladies' fashion. It was also host to most of the city's sewing machine sellers, for this was an era when the majority of women made their own garments. Although most of the men's tailors were in the financial district a block or so away, a few men's haberdashers such as S. N. Moody, Walshe's, and H. B. Stevens were on Canal near the intersection of St. Charles.

S. J. Shwartz, renamed Maison Blanche in 1897, beat Holmes in becoming the city's first full-line department store. It was touted as a "New York-style department store." Its five floors were packed with

During the Christmas season, shoppers and their children would stop at the window of Maison Blanche to see the popular Mr. Bingle marionette show. (Courtesy of the family of Emile Alline, Sr.)

merchandise, including the latest fashions and modern housewares. The store had about 150 feet of big show windows along Canal Street. By the time the store opened, electricity was common in the commercial district and MB's windows, which were lined with mirrors lit by hundreds of bare light bulbs—the fad in store design at the time—that not only showed merchandise to full advantage both day and night, but threw rays of bright light into nighttime Canal Street.

Not wishing to be left behind, D. H. Holmes doubled its Canal Street frontage in 1898 and built an addition along the back of the store on Iberville Street in 1904. There were other department stores coming along the thoroughfare such as Krauss at Basin Street; Fellman's, which became Feibleman's at Carondelet; and Marks Isaacs

Before the debut of marionette shows featuring Mr. Bingle, the perky snowman that became Maison Blanche's "mascot," the Canal Street department store presented themed windows such as this 1945 Christmas display featuring a circus. (Courtesy of the family of Emile Alline, Sr.)

in the Touro block. As ready-made clothing became not only of higher quality but respectable, fashionable clothing stores such as Godchaux's and Kreeger's expanded, and Gus Mayer, Rubenstein Brothers, Keller-Zander, and Mayer Israel emerged. Some were in business on Canal Street into the 1980s; Rubensteins is still in business. Numerous jewelry stores such as Hyde and Goodrich, Tyler's, Schooler's, and Hausmann's also called Canal Street home. All but one, Adler's, are gone.

As stores grew so did their show window displays. From haphazard arrangements of merchandise in the 1850s, displays grew more organized and elegant as the century moved on. During Christmas of 1884, according to the *Daily Picayune,* Canal Street was "gaily decorated, ablaze with light, with the mammoth stores displaying fairy treasures to delight passers-by." Two years later the *Picayune* reported that store clerks vied with each other on Christmas Eve to see who could arrange the most attractive display, while "every bit of fancy goods was shown [which were] visions of delight." At Christmas 1890 the *Picayune* boasted that "artistic enterprise has made the line of [Canal Street] show windows wondrously beautiful."

Christmas Gift Giving and Advertising

The exchange of Christmas gifts has long been part of the Christian holiday season. Prior to the nineteenth century, gifts tended to be small remembrances. In the late eighteenth and early nineteenth centuries, newspapers might mention Christmas giving—or Xmas gifts, since at the time X was an acceptable term using the Greek letter *chi* as a symbol

This Christmas display presented by Maison Blanche in the early 1940s depicts the Old Woman Who Lived in a Shoe but also promoted the store's supply of dolls. (Courtesy of the family of Emile Alline, Sr.)

of the first letter of Christ's name—but there was little if any effort to encourage the exchange of gifts.

Stores, such as those in New Orleans, were small and specialized; their advertisements were equally small. In the newspapers of the day, ads were not more than a column wide and at most an inch or two down the page. As stores increased in size and number—and competition grew stiffer—advertising expanded accordingly.

In the 1860s stores started expressing special Christmas sentiments. Words such as "Christmas" and "holiday" enhanced the still un-illustrated ads to catch the reader's eye. Some New Orleans stores included "New Year" in their advertisements. In 1866, F. G. Barriere, relocated from the French Quarter to Canal Street, advertised both Christmas and New Year's gifts. Eyrich's, the elegant book dealer and stationer, also advertised gifts for the season, while the Canal Street jeweler A. B. Griswold advertised "Holiday Gifts." Such holiday sentiments would have been difficult to find in Christmas advertising in New Orleans just twenty years earlier.

By 1869 the number of references to Christmas in advertising had grown significantly. The elegant dressmaker Madame Olympe advertised that she had brought new goods from Paris "especially for Christmas and New Year's gifts." Kreeger's, a ladies' shop then on Magazine Street, stocked "new goods, selected for the Christmas holidays." Payton and Zebal in the St. Charles Hotel simply declared, "HO! For the Holidays."

In 1869, Guéblé & Nippert was especially ambitious when the store advertised its abundant stock and quality in its toy department in an eleven stanza poem, some of which reads:

Emile Alline, Sr., longtime display director for Maison Blanche, created what he called a "snowdoll" as the store's Christmas mascot, and Mr. Bingle was born. (Courtesy of the family of Emile Alline, Sr.)

Would you thus your children bless—
On their little hearts impress
A whole life of happiness
And of joy—
Help now their gladsome mirth
As they gather round your hearth,
Nor let there be a dearth
Of their toys.

Now all these, and more, you'll meet
At Guéblé's Toy Retreat,
One Thirty Seven Canal Street,
Where one gets
All that boys and girls admire—
All that Ma and Pa desire
For their pets.

Stores were beginning to advertise specialized seasonal items. In 1884, Alphonse Marx on Dryades Street highlighted its "Christmas Cards and Souvenirs," while bookseller Eyrich's touted, "Our line of Prang's Christmas and New Year's Cards . . . We have some exquisite

General News
Society

The Times-Picayune

Classified
Financial

SECTION THREE   NEW ORLEANS, FRIDAY, NOVEMBER 6, 1953   PAGE THIRTY-FIVE

During the 1960s, one Maison Blanche promotion during the Christmas season was the "arrival" of Mr. Bingle and Santa Claus via Eastern Airlines. (Courtesy of the family of Emille Alline, Sr. and the Times-Picayune)

Truman Capote's Canal Street Christmas

Even though he was born in New Orleans in 1924, author Truman Capote didn't spend much time in his birthplace. After his parents divorced, his early years were spent in rural Alabama with cousins.

His childhood memory of traveling by bus to New Orleans to visit his father, Archulus "Arch" Persons, whom he barely knew, is the focus of *One Christmas*, which he wrote in the 1980s.

The day before Christmas, we were walking along Canal Street. I stopped dead still, mesmerized by a magical object that I saw in the window of a big toy store. It was a model airplane large enough to sit in and pedal like a bicycle. It was green and had a red propeller. I was convinced that if you pedaled fast enough it would take off and fly!

On Christmas Day, Capote found other presents under the tree from his father, but not the airplane.

I reminded him of the airplane we had seen in the toy store on Canal Street. His face sagged. Oh, yes, he remembered the airplane and how expensive it was. Nevertheless, the next day I was sitting in that airplane dreaming I was zooming toward heaven while my father wrote out a check for a happy salesman.

Caroline Jane Scott displays her pair of Bingles, just unwrapped on Christmas morning. (Courtesy of Stacey and Kurt Scott)

Hand-painted cards, very elegant." In 1886, Wharton's on Canal Street at Carondelet Street sold cards priced from 1½¢ to $15, an astonishing amount at the time, showing that by the mid-1880s, New Orleans had regained its prosperity after the end of Reconstruction. For many people there was enough wealth to celebrate a Merry Christmas.

By 1885, D. H. Holmes and other Canal Street stores strung electric lines throughout their buildings. As electricity became more and more common in the commercial area, building owners and merchants decorated their show windows with electric lights and began decorating their exteriors at Christmas and Mardi Gras. The impact of lights became especially popular after the spectacular effects of lighting at the 1884 World's Fair, held on the grounds of what today is Audubon Park.

At Christmas, Canal Street soon became a fairyland of twinkling lights and each year light and window displays became more lavish. The decorations gave people another reason to make their way to the street on Christmas Eve, since this was when the lights were switched on to start the season.

In this photograph from the 1960s, two Mr. Bingles are perched above the Canal Street entrance to Maison Blanche. (Courtesy of the family of Emile Alline, Sr.)

From the 1940s through 1979, this four-story cutout Santa Claus figure in front of Sears and Roebuck, just a block off Canal Street at the corner of Common and Baronne Streets, was a familiar sight during the Christmas season. (Photo by C. F. Weber, courtesy of Bergeron Gallery)

Taking a photograph with Santa at a downtown department store was a holiday ritual. In this photograph from the early 1960s, New Orleanian Monica Barthé Turner sits with the Santa from Maison Blanche while Mr. Bingle hovers overhead. Turner recalls: "I just remember how the wait was long, and the line to see Santa seemed endless. All the kids were dressed so nice and the moms and dads kept reminding them how their behavior would make a big difference to Santa when he gave out the toys. Of course some kids would still fidget and need reprimanding, and we'd look up at my mother, who was looking back at us with those eyes that said, 'You'd better not try that.' When we got closer and could actually see Santa, the carnage was everywhere. Kids who had been in line giving their parents a hard time were collapsing in terror or liquefying on Santa's lap. With all the screaming and pulling away, you would think it was the vaccination clinic. Ribbons, barrettes, and bow ties were flying and rosy cheeks were full of tears and spit. Parents left in disgust—either embarrassed because of their child's behavior or blaming the store for the length of time in line. Again we'd look up at my mother, who was looking back at us with those eyes that said, 'You'd better not try that.' Since we were more afraid of her than Santa, we didn't and here's the picture to prove it." (Courtesy of Monica Barthé Turner)

Christmas Eve Shopping

One of the enticements of Canal Street on Christmas Eve was that many of the holiday window decorations were being shown for the first time during the season. (At this time the celebration of the season began on the day before Christmas rather than at Thanksgiving. Stores in New Orleans did not even begin advertising Christmas and New Year's gifts until mid-December, and most shoppers delayed their buying forays until Christmas Eve or after.) By the 1880s store window displays were wonderlands of greenery, ribbons, and other ephemera of the season. With the advent of electric lighting the windows became even more magical.

The mob of potential shoppers on Christmas Eve prompted merchants to keep their stores open late, in some cases even after 1 A.M., only to reopen early on Christmas Day. Often people did not begin shopping until Christmas Eve. For some businesses Christmas Eve was payday, and families with children in tow joined other merrymakers, going from store to store and from one store Santa to the next. By then store Santas were becoming a common sight.

Outside the stores were street vendors displaying notions, ribbons, balloons, clothing items, and even birds for sale. Many vendors specialized in noisemakers, drums, horns, and firecrackers, all to contribute to making as much racket as possible.

As Christmas Eve on Canal Street progressed toward the evening, the types of crowds changed. Right after sunset most of the people were shoppers. As a louder crowd began to descend, the shoppers abandoned the street for home or Midnight Mass. Late at night the sightseeing crowd came to Canal Street, and many were very well dressed. They were there to promenade, to see and to be seen, which was a popular part of the celebration. No matter the time of night, the beat on the street continued.

By the mid-nineteenth century, offices and businesses were starting to close early on Christmas Eve and, for some, all day Christmas Day. Even the newspapers took the day off. In 1871 the *Daily Picayune* noted, "To allow our employés and compositors to enjoy the Christmas holiday no paper will be issued." By this time most public offices closed as well. "The public servant and the private citizen alike appreciate the holiday," said the *Picayune*. This was not true of the poor shop assistants, stock clerks, or delivery boys who more than ever had to serve the needs of the ever-growing Christmas-gift-giving public.

This Maison Blanche Santa from the late 1950s seems very willing to listen to what's on the Christmas list. (Courtesy of Peggy Scott Laborde)

Mickey Barthelemy, wife of former New Orleans mayor Sidney J. Barthelemy (who served from 1986-94), promoted citywide Christmas celebrations, including a parade. She is shown here with internationally known New Orleans chef Paul Prudhomme as Santa. (Louisiana Division/City Archives, New Orleans Public Library)

Mayor and Mrs. Victor H. Schiro pose with Santa Claus, 1966. Schiro served as mayor of New Orleans from 1961-70. He and wife, Sunny, often participated in public events. (Louisiana Division/City Archives, New Orleans Public Library)

This snowy scene above the entrance to Krauss department store may have left some New Orleanians hoping for a flurry. (Courtesy of Hugo Kahn)

Among the most lavish and popular displays at Christmas was the almost three-hundred-foot-long lobby of the Roosevelt (later Fairmont and once again Roosevelt) Hotel. Flocked trees and a canopy of "angel hair" batting covered with ornaments created a winter wonderland. This photograph is from the 1960s. The tradition was discontinued in 1966 due to fire safety regulations, but with the advent of flame retardant decorations, this popular tradition was revived in 1994. (Courtesy of the Fairmont Hotel)

The St. Charles Hotel, known by the early 1970s as the Sheraton Charles, decorated its lobby at Christmastime with colored lights and flocked trees. (Courtesy R. R. "Tim" Richardson, Canton, Ohio)

For many years Betty Finnin, the official decorator for the City of New Orleans, and her staff adorned the Canal Street lampposts for Christmas and Mardi Gras. (Louisiana Division/City Archives, New Orleans Public Library)

Late Christmas Eve hours were slowly eliminated, especially since by the late 1880s street crowds were getting more rowdy and boisterous, more in a mood to revel than to shop. As early as 1886, D. H. Holmes advertised, "For the convenience of our customers Our Store will open . . . Until 9 O'Clock. " In this expanding age of social conscience, there was finally a growing concern about the welfare of store workers. Stores started adding more staff to relieve stress on the full-time clerks, and in 1895, S. J. Shwartz doubled its sales staff for Christmas sales. In 1904, A. Schwartz announced that it would close at 6 P.M., and D. H. Holmes not only closed early, but also advertised that it would remain closed on Christmas Day, "To give our employees a needed rest."

City of New Orleans decorator Betty Finnin was in charge of an annual Christmas parade in the 1950s. From left, Fred Green, Mrs. William R. Robinson, and Finnin put the finishing touches on a float. (Photograph by Photography Unlimited, Louisiana Division/City Archives, New Orleans Public Library)

Canal Street: "The Battleground"

Canal Street was not only the center of Christmas shopping, but it was also dubbed the "battleground," as the late-night Christmas Eve revels engulfed it with noise and mayhem that had long been a part of the holiday season in New Orleans. By the mid-1860s, as Canal Street became the city's great gathering place, more and more Christmas Eve activity gravitated there, which was different from the antebellum period when there was no particular center of Christmas Eve revelry. Canal Street was already a focus of life and shopping in New Orleans, and at Christmas it was even more enticing with its

From the 1870s into the early twentieth century, retailers gave away colorful trade cards as promotions. This one from the 1880s depicts a Christmas angel from the French Market Tea Depot on St. Ann Street in the French Quarter. (The Historic New Orleans Collection)

smartly dressed window decorations and, later, electric light displays.

As soon as the sun set on Christmas Eve, thousands of people made their way to Canal Street. They came on foot, by streetcar, or by carriage. The crowd knew no class barrier. Many people promenaded in their finery. The occasional shoeless urchin and hoodlum were also part of the mix.

Christmas in New Orleans was announced by the incessant blare of tin and paper horns sold by fashionable shops and street vendors. Part of the milieu was the beat of drums and the boom and blast of fireworks. In spite of complaints from the police and prominent business leaders, fireworks danced and hissed on the streets, causing the uninitiated to jump and leap in fright. Of even greater danger were falling bullets. There were individuals who used Christmas Eve as an excuse to indiscriminately shoot firearms, to the detriment of those unsuspecting people who might get caught in the line of fire. There were every year numerous injuries and even deaths brought about by this practice.

Bands of Christmas merrymakers strolled along Canal Street for hours after sunset. Large parties of young adults rushed through the crowds tooting horns at everybody, creating lots of noise throughout the night and Christmas Day. The *Daily Picayune* called it "Babel and pandemonium and fairyland combined." Many other people less intent on noisemaking went downtown to witness with delight and occasional horror the incessant late-night show.

On Christmas Eve 1884, an enterprising group of young men tried to astound everybody when they fashioned a giant horn over five feet long designed to make the biggest noise ever. They carried it along Canal Street taking turns blowing into its several mouthpieces. The oversized horn proved to be more fearful looking than loud since its noise could not be heard above the din.

Such noisemaking and mayhem on Christmas Eve was not unique to New Orleans, although in the United States it was more associated with New Orleans than with other large cities. As a warm-climate city without extreme December weather, New Orleans lent itself more readily to such winter activities. In 1884 the *Daily Picayune* said, "The New Orleans Christmas is becoming as celebrated and distinctive as the New Orleans Carnival. Strangers concede to the Crescent City a talent for enjoyment . . . and generosity in its exercise." In this World's Fair year with more winter visitors than usual in town, the *Picayune* noted that

By the 1890s, Canal Street had been New Orleans' main shopping district for over half a century. It was especially busy during the Christmas season, as seen in this newspaper photograph. (Louisiana Division/City Archives, New Orleans Public Library)

Stocked for Christmas, the toy department at D. H. Holmes was pictured in the New Orleanian *magazine of December 15, 1930. (The Historic New Orleans Collection)*

This Maison Blanche ad from a December 1907 Times Democrat doesn't provide an address for the department store. Everyone knew it was on Canal Street. (Louisiana Division/City Archives, New Orleans Public Library)

"strangers within the city gates Christmas Eve and Christmas Day found . . . a great deal of discordant noise." The *Daily Picayune* repeated its opinion in 1890 when it stated, "New Orleans has a characteristic Christmas as well as a unique carnival. Canal Street has always been the main battleground for the elements of discord that marked the celebration."

But across New Orleans there was the growing feeling that time and changing tastes were finally tempering the worst features of the city's Christmas revelry. Starting in the 1890s bands of young men descended on Canal Street on Christmas Eve, but they did not carry guns or firecrackers. They were on missions of mirth; they paraded and sang as long as they were able to survive the night and the "good cheer" dispensed by households and businesses that welcomed their friendly form of merriment. Some of the singing groups wore military or marching uniforms and carried banners and blazing torches to announce their arrival. The *Daily Picayune* commented that they carried "flames and fire of a harmless sort."

In 1904 the *Picayune* reported the Christmas Eve activities of a young nurse who worked at Touro Infirmary. When the young lady got off duty in the early evening, she and friends made their way to Canal Street to take in the requisite sights. The group then went to the theater, after which they went to supper—a *réveillon*—at a Canal Street restaurant. Later they drove up St. Charles Avenue to the home of Dr. Rudolph Matas, the noted medical researcher, where they serenaded him into the evening.

Prior to World War I, Canal Street was still jammed with revelers on Christmas Eve, but the activities became more subdued. The crowds continued to surge back and forth good-naturedly blowing horns and ringing bells, but the shooting of guns and fireworks and the resultant injuries were diminishing on Christmas only to eventually crop up on New Year's Eve. Public protest was becoming more vocal about fireworks and the indiscriminant shooting of firearms. While these acts had been discouraged for years, police rarely interfered with them until the twentieth century, when laws were enacted and lawbreakers subject to arrest.

In 1923 the New Orleans superintendent of police cautioned citizens against allowing their Christmas exuberance to take the form of firing guns. In spite of the warning, people were wounded by careless celebrants, although the numbers were far lower than those of forty years earlier. Front-page headlines in the Christmas issue of the *New Orleans States* summed the situation up when it said, "2 Stabbed Many Hurt In Sunday [Christmas Eve] Revels."

Increasingly more lavish show window displays and spectacular electric lighting helped lure the attention of the masses away from fireworks, but fewer Canal Street stores remained open on Christmas. As the use of fireworks diminished, Canal was no longer the "battleground" that it had been just a decade earlier and revelers looked for other places to vent their energies. Many went to the nearby

During the late nineteenth century large Christmas Eve crowds converged on Canal Street blowing horns, beating drums, and shooting fireworks. In 1884, Frank Leslie's Illustrated Newspaper *depicted a group of young men who fashioned a giant horn in an unsuccessful attempt to outdo other noisemakers. (The Historic New Orleans Collection)*

"Tango Belt" along Iberville Street in the French Quarter, where there were small hotels, restaurants, dance halls, and honky-tonks.

During World War I there was a lull in Christmas celebrations and an abrupt end to most of the noisy events, but Christmas Eve 1917 was welcomed in by thousands of people in Lafayette Square singing carols and listening to speeches that mixed religion and patriotism. Mayor Martin Behrman called it "a splendid thought that we should have this community singing and a tree to greet Christmas." Before the caroling began an eighty-seven-year-old woman flicked the switch that lit the tree and "a star topping its radiance." For many years a Christmas tree was put up in Lafayette Square.

The following year, the death and sorrow of the Great War was compounded by the October 1918 great influenza epidemic. With over three thousand victims of the "Spanish Flu" in New Orleans alone, Christmas, in spite of the November 11 end of the war, was subdued.

In its Christmas edition of 1922 the *New Orleans States* headlined, "Christmas Observed By People At Home." Crowds still made their way into the streets, but the behavior wasn't as boisterous as it had once been. People caroled on Canal Street and in Lafayette Square as well as throughout neighborhoods. Restaurants and hotel ballrooms

As shown in this 1884 Harper's Weekly, in addition to shopping, creating a ruckus on Canal Street was considered a part of holiday activities during the Christmas season. (From the collection of Peggy Scott Laborde)

were filled to capacity with revelers. Churches were packed for both Midnight Mass and for Protestant services. On Christmas Day the poor were fed and orphans were given gifts, but downtown, the streets were practically deserted. "On Christmas Day itself," according to the *States*, "it centered in the homes of New Orleans. For that's where Christmas belongs. At the home hearthstone."

Another blow to the Canal Street celebrations came with Prohibition. Drinking had long been a part of the Christmas celebration. In most cases it was just part of the conviviality of the season. In 1866 after the office of the *Daily Picayune* closed down on Christmas Eve, "[the staff] began our Christmas right early . . . due to the courtesy of Col. E.F. Duncan, of the St. James Hotel barroom . . . who sent us so bountiful an eggnog and such good wine." The indiscriminate shooting of guns and resultant injuries was often blamed on drunkenness.

The 1920s ban against the consumption of alcohol took its toll on public display at Christmas, and many revelers celebrated indoors. In 1923 the *Times-Picayune* noted that "Christmas and the flowing bowl are so closely associated in the minds of some folks" and reported on a man who strolled into a post office—perhaps thinking it a speakeasy—with bottles of wine under each arm. Spied by a federal agent, he was arrested and spent Christmas Eve "getting a bondsman." In 1928 the *States* reported, "Xmas Booze Is Plentiful," and it flowed freely on Christmas Eve, resulting in numerous arrests for intoxication. Nearly every restaurant and "soft drink stand" was reportedly selling liquor.

The massive amount of pedestrian traffic that was part of Christmas in the nineteenth century was replaced by increasing automobile traffic in the first decades of the twentieth century. Forty extra policemen were put on duty in 1922 not only to regulate the increased flow of Christmas traffic, but also to be on the lookout for intoxicated drivers. In 1928 the *New Orleans Item* reported that traffic mishaps with injuries began Christmas Eve and continued into the next day. Such incidents became as common as the gunshot wounds that were still prevalent through the 1920s.

The stock market crash of 1929 and the Depression of the 1930s further eroded traditional public Christmas revels in New Orleans. In 1931 the streets remained relatively quiet, and the *Item* said, "This year the celebration was a little more solemn than usual." According to the newspaper it was a day of "Good will toward men," as the emphasis was on helping the poor, making sure that every person had a Christmas dinner and that every child got a toy. Scores of charitable programs provided dinners and food baskets for those in need. The deepening Depression was evident at the Doll and Toy Fund presentation in

This advertisement for Bernard and Grunning, once one of New Orleans' leading jewelers, appeared in the New Orleanian *magazine of December 15, 1930. Eight years later the store crafted the gold monstrance for the Eucharistic Congress held in New Orleans that year. (The Historic New Orleans Collection)*

Christmas catalogs such as this 1952 edition from D. H. Holmes have helped promote retailers and the Christmas buying season since the late nineteenth century. (The Historic New Orleans Collection)

Heinemann Baseball Park where twenty thousand white children showed up to be followed by ten thousand black children.

While after World War I, Canal Street may no longer have been *the* place to be on Christmas Eve or Christmas Day, it remained the chief destination between Thanksgiving and Christmas. Although there were other shopping districts such as Dryades Street and Magazine Street, Canal Street was the showplace. Here were the best window displays, the best merchandise, including big toy departments and Santas. Canal Street had been that way since the Civil War, and it continued in that position until the 1980s when suburban shopping centers, which started small in New Orleans in the 1950s, finally won out in enticing shoppers.

Photo by E. Claudel

On Christmas Day, Catholic families visited church crèches or "cribs." Among the largest and most impressive was that at the Jesuit Church of the Immaculate Conception on Baronne Street, depicted in the Sunday Illustrated *Magazine of the* Daily Picayune *in 1910. (The Historic New Orleans Collection)*

CHAPTER TWO

The Early Days

New Orleans' First Christmas

The first observance of Christmas in New Orleans must have been a joyous one, even for the struggling little settlement of fifty European men who, along with the local Indians, toiled daily felling trees, digging ditches, building houses, and just trying to survive in an inhospitable land. As darkness descended on Christmas Eve and the men were allowed to rest until the day after Christmas, they began celebrating what in eighteenth-century France was cherished as the holiest night of the year. The tiny, less than a year-old settlement of New Orleans celebrated its first Christmas in 1718. Growth had been slow and the land where the French Quarter now stands was merely a clearing. It had only four buildings: a house for its founder, Jean Baptiste Le Moyne Sieur de Bienville; a warehouse; a barracks for the soldiers and builders who made up its European population; and a Catholic church. The colony was strictly Roman Catholic since that was the official religion of of France, the settlement's mother country. In addition to commerce, another goal of the colony was the religious conversion of the resident native Indians.

The small church, like the other buildings in the settlement, was crudely constructed of cypress logs. The roof was thatched with palmetto leaves, which offered only scant protection from the chilly rain that was reported to have fallen throughout the day. Early accounts noted that as midnight arrived, the men, along with a few Indian converts, filed into the little church for Midnight Mass.

The officiating priest, probably a soldier-priest who worked as diligently as everyone else building houses, donned his clerical robes for this all-important service. Flickering shadows were cast across the faces of the worshippers by the candles on the tiny altar.

The only other decoration on the altar would have been most likely a small crèche consisting of figures of the Christ child in the crib, the Virgin Mary, St. Joseph, and perhaps a donkey. By 1718 the crèche, or crib, was the most beloved part of Catholic Christmas and was a must even in the most modest of circumstances. Crèches were included in Christmas services in Rome as far back as the fourth century and by the eighth century were an integral part of the celebration. The crèche's popularity increased in 1223, when on Christmas Eve, St. Francis of Assisi staged

Nativity scenes such as this one at St. Louis Cathedral in the 1930s have long been a part of the Christmas celebration and were popularized by St. Francis of Assisi in the 1200s. (The Historic New Orleans Collection)

a living Nativity. The depiction of the manger and the Holy Family, whether live or in sculpture, spread across Europe and became an integral part of the celebration, even in colonial outposts.

For virtually all eighteenth-century Christians, Christmas was also a day of secular activities. Nobility enjoyed watching and participating in masques, a presentation that involved music, dancing, singing, and acting. There were also elaborate festivals and parades, along with gambling, drinking, playing pranks, and rowdy street fun for everybody else. After the Protestant Reformation, in some countries, such as Scotland and in America's New England, non-pious Christmas activities were considered an anathema and the holiday fell into disfavor and was even banned in some locations.

In Catholic France and her colonies such intolerance was not the case, nor would it have been so in 1718 New Orleans, where a day off work would have been a welcome respite from the drudgery of clearing and construction. During New Orleans' first Christmas Day there would have been gambling with dice and cards. Men would have played pranks on each other, since this is what would have been done in France, and they would have sung carols into the night.

The amount of eating and drinking at most European Christmases was mind-boggling, with gargantuan multicourse meals that were consumed along with tankards of wine and beer. In 1718, New Orleans was no exception. Indians provided vegetables and grain. Wild game was abundant for a Christmas feast: there were deer, quail, snipe, duck, oysters, shrimp, crawfish, and most notably *dindons de guinee*, wild turkeys. These birds were found throughout Louisiana and so plentiful that when they roosted in live oak trees their collective weight would bend the stout tree limbs. There was an abundance of drink, since several days before Christmas the good ship *Neptune* was reported to have docked in front of the settlement on the Mississippi River laden with casks of red and white wines and brandy. Gambling, eating, and drinking were the order of the day at this first New Orleans Nöel, recalling memories of home.

The Church of St. Louis: The Center of Christmas

Life was difficult in early New Orleans. It was isolated, money was short, and certain foods were sometimes hard to come by. Spring of 1719 brought serious flooding from the Mississippi River, and in 1722 a hurricane leveled most of the town. Christmas celebrations from one December to the next in the early years would have been little different from the first one: an escape from daily toil.

In spite of the problems, the settlers were making progress. The population was expanding, as European women, including the Ursuline nuns, began arriving. In 1719 the first African slaves were brought in. Germans were encouraged to come to the area and became successful farmers, helping to feed the colony. Many settled upriver from New Orleans. Their new home was eventually referred to as "Des Allemandes," or the German Coast.

The center of New Orleans society, and all of its eighteenth-century Christmas observances, was its church. The first rustic church building where the Christmas of 1718 was celebrated disappeared to history, probably a victim of the devastating 1722 hurricane. In that same year a visitor, Jesuit historian Fr. François Xavier de Charlevoix, described half of a wretched warehouse serving as a makeshift church. The next year the town's house of worship was moved to a former tavern on the Mississippi riverfront.

In the early 1720s services took place in a newly constructed military barracks. By 1723 efforts to build a pleasant and permanent church for the citizens of New Orleans were finally coming together. The town's official plan by Adrien de Pauger called for a church facing the Mississippi River on the Place d'Armes, now Jackson Square, where the St. Louis Cathedral stands today.

De Pauger designed in 1721 the first structure actually planned as a church. It was dedicated to Louis IX, the sainted king of France. Originally intended to be constructed from timber, by the time construction began a brickyard had been established in New Orleans. The house of worship would consist of brick foundation piers and brick between post walls, a French technique of half-timbering called *briqueté entre poteaux.* One of the town's most substantial buildings, its outer walls were covered with protective plaster and buttressed with timber beams for stability. The church was dedicated just before Christmas 1727, when the town was not quite ten years old.

The original Church of St. Louis, its dedication as a cathedral still decades away, was cruciform in shape. The building was 112 feet long, 32 feet wide, and 24 feet high. Over the front doorway was a small

In this drawing by Henry W. Krotzer, Jr., the Place d'Armes, now Jackson Square, appears as it would have in the 1720s soon after construction of the first Church of St. Louis. (The Historic New Orleans Collection)

belfry with two bells and a clock that struck the hour. Inside there were eighteen pews, their use auctioned off to the highest bidders, as well as additional seating for the Supreme Council and chairs for the governor and the intendant (a holder of a public administrative office). For other worshippers it was standing room only unless one brought a chair.

At last there was a permanent church to function as the center of both religious and social life for the town's growing community. Midnight Mass and Christmas could be celebrated in style. Throughout the eighteenth century, services in New Orleans were impressive. Early on the Church of St. Louis had the luxuries of an organ and an accomplished choir.

In 1751 mezzanines were added so that more worshippers could be accommodated, but just twelve years later the building was temporarily shut down. The city's damp climate had taken its toll, rendering the church in a deplorable condition. For a while services were moved to a royal warehouse on Dumaine Street where a wall was removed to create a hall large enough to accommodate the congregation. Once repairs were made the church reopened for services.

This structure served the community's religious needs for only sixty Christmases. On March 21, 1788, Good Friday, a candle accidentally ignited drapes in a house on Chartres Street. Soon the house was engulfed in flames that quickly spread to neighboring buildings. By nightfall 856 buildings were gone. In what must have seemed like the blink of an eye, four-fifths of New Orleans was in ruins.

Among those charred structures was the Church of St. Louis, which remained essentially untouched for almost a year after the fire. Mass was moved to various spots: the Government House, built in 1761 on Levee (now Decatur) Street at Toulouse; Charity Hospital on Rampart Street; and the Ursuline Convent on Chartres Street, yet another survivor of the fire that remains standing today, though somewhat altered.

In 1789 construction began on a replacement church. Services were held next door in a temporary building erected where the Cabildo is today. The new church was financed by Don Andrés Almonester y Roxas, a native of Andalusia, Spain. One of New Orleans' wealthiest property owners, he owned the lands around the Place d'Armes, now Jackson Square. Don Gilberto Guillemard, a Frenchman in the military service of Spain, designed the new house of worship. (After the end of the French and Indian War in 1763 control of Louisiana shifted from France to Spain.) The new building was horizontal, low, and flat-roofed in an architectural style more typically Spanish than French. As New Orleans was rebuilt after the fire, Spanish building design became a major influence in New Orleans architecture, evident in surviving eighteenth-century French Quarter buildings.

The new church was built of brick and covered with plaster that was painted to resemble marble. On either side of its front facade were two low towers topped with bell-shaped roofs. Inside, the floor and altar were of marble, and paintings and sculpture adorned the walls. It was obvious that New Orleans was growing in size and wealth since its new church was not only larger than its predecessor, but also grander. This more impressive building was also befitting of the new and expanded role the church was about to play, as the sprawling Spanish territories of Louisiana and the Floridas had been designated a diocese.

On December 8, 1794, a second fire swept through New Orleans, this time destroying almost two hundred buildings. Although losses included the temporary church, miraculously the newly finished edifice was spared the fiery fate of its predecessor. It was dedicated at an opulent Midnight Mass on Christmas Eve, 1794. It was now called St. Louis Cathedral.

Celebrating Christmas in Colonial New Orleans

The celebration of Christmas Eve in New Orleans in 1794 was a far cry from Christmas Eve seventy-six years earlier. From fifty European men and a few local Indians the town had grown into a wealthy trading community of around seventy-five hundred. Almost half were of African descent. About half of this population was enslaved and the other half free. There were also Germans, along with a few Anglo-Americans and Jews. These newcomers were drawn by opportunities for increased trade coming down the Mississippi River from the United States west of the Appalachian Mountains. Although New Orleans was ruled by Spain, French language and customs persevered. Roman Catholicism remained the legal religion and there was still only one church. Local tolerance tended to disregard differences as diversity flourished. The small city may have been isolated from other population centers, but its wealth and trade connections helped make it worldlier than one might expect. In spite of the city's unpaved streets, life in New Orleans could be surprisingly elegant and fashionable.

European and Catholic traditions still dominated the Christmas season in New Orleans and just as the rude log hut of 1718 was the center of that year's solemn rituals, the fine new St. Louis Cathedral was the center of Christmas rites in the last years of colonial rule. As in Europe, Midnight Mass was not the only holiday event that was observed in New Orleans. A more gregarious, secular side included the usual pranks, noise, and street revels that had long been an integral part of Christmas and would remain part of the New Orleans celebration throughout the nineteenth century.

A short story titled "Clopin-Clopant" by Marie Louise Points appeared in the *Daily Picayune* on Christmas Day in 1892. A charming bit of holiday fiction, it gives a glimpse at some of the Christmas Eve activities in New Orleans in its final colonial days before the Louisiana Purchase in 1803.

On Christmas Eve there was an "undertone of happiness," writes Points, "for all day long music and laughter echoed from the old brick buildings. . . . *Belles demoiselles* loitered among the roses and jasmines of the courtyards, twining bouquets and planning for the *réveillon*, which every Creole home from that day to this holds on Christmas Eve."

Throughout the day the streets were filled with "fun loving people"

The official exchange of French and American flags after the Louisiana Purchase took place five days before Christmas, 1803, in the Place d'Armes (now Jackson Square). (The Historic New Orleans Collection)

who laughed and shared greetings of the season. It was also a magical time for mischievous boys, and Points' story revolves around a group of youngsters who went out to celebrate with tin horns, firecrackers, and other noisemakers. Gunshots were among the sounds that welcomed in the season. Christmas "meant for them a carnival of mischief. There was noise, there was banging on doors," all to disturb the peace of folks who preferred a more peaceful, reverential holiday.

One especially fun-loving youngster in the story, the ringleader of the band, is not far from fact and reveals how playful and rowdy Christmas Eve was in the years around 1800 and would remain for the rest of the century. The ringleader and his friends "slipped into the . . . Cathedral . . . and filled one holy water font with ink and the other with crabs, so that all the *belles demoiselles* might make black crosses on their foreheads when they took the *eau-benie* [holy water] or scream with terror when the crabs bit their pretty fingers as they piously dipped them in the *benitie* [holy water font]." From a safe distance the pranksters roared with laughter, and continuing with their mission of misbehavior, they gathered up "tin-pans, bones, old fiddles, horns and accordions to make a din, at the expense of everyone they passed," and shouted to other urchins to come and join them in their holiday revels.

The Louisiana Purchase

New Orleans' time as a colony ended in 1803 with the Louisiana Purchase. The United States sought to purchase the city and wound up obtaining the vast Territory of Louisiana from France. This transaction insured that Americans living west of the Appalachians would continue to have access to the port of New Orleans, their only outlet to the sea, for trading purposes. The resulting purchase doubled the size of the young nation. France had already taken Louisiana back from Spain in 1800; however, the official transfer from Spain to France did not occur take place until November 30, 1803. The United States had purchased the territory months prior to the November date, but not until December 20, 1803, did France officially cede the territory to the Americans in ceremonies in the Place d'Armes.

Louisiana's colonial history came to a close during the Christmas and New Year's season of 1803-4. The result was one of the most high-spirited holiday seasons in the Crescent City's history, as balls and parties, activities dear to the city's heart, went on for nearly two months.

William C. C. Claiborne, the first American governor of Louisiana, wrote that people in New Orleans loved to dance, and C. C. Robin, a visitor to Louisiana from 1803 to 1805, said, "Winter is the season of balls and they are very frequent."

In a letter to James Madison on January 2, 1804, Governor Claiborne wrote, "This is the season of Festivity here, and I am pleased to find that the change in Government has given additional Spirit to the public amusements." And amusing it was—all-night balls, parties, fireworks displays, parades, and other festivities left an indelible mark on local Christmas celebrations for years to come.

Among the highlights of 1803 were balls given by French, Spanish, and American officials, all of whom tried to outdo each other. Festivities began on November 30, 1803, when throngs of people watched as Spanish governor Manuel de Salcedo and former governor the Marqués de Casa Calvo turned Louisiana over to the French colonial prefect Pierre Clément Laussat at ceremonies in the Place d'Armes.

Pierre Clément Laussat, who was sent by France to accept the colony from Spain and then transfer it to the United States, recalled that a "continuous holiday" began on November 30. A dinner was given the following day for officials and seventy-five guests. It lasted until 7 A.M. the next day, although some stragglers remembered leaving at 10 A.M. Gambling, another local passion, continued until at least 8 A.M. Floods of candlelight illuminated the elegant guests and their surroundings, while music filled the air with such popular dances as the French and English quadrilles and gallopades. Laussat wrote that the women present were all "beautiful or pretty and all of them well

The plantation home of Bernard de Marigny was at one time the residence of French colonial prefect Pierre Clément Laussat, who transferred Louisiana to the United States. The house was the venue for some of the lavish balls surrounding the transfer during the Christmas holiday season of 1803. (The Historic New Orleans Collection)

built, elegant and gorgeously dressed." There were congratulatory speeches and three toasts made—one to Napoleon, another to King Carlos of Spain, and one to American president Thomas Jefferson. From this successful and festive event an informal challenge was made prompting diplomatic dignitaries to stage balls honoring each other.

The Marqués de Casa Calvo gave the first ball in honor of Laussat and his wife Marie-Anne Peborde Laussat on December 8, 1803. Dining, dancing, and gambling again lasted until the wee hours. The Laussats were not to be outdone, and on December 15 they gave a ball in honor of Casa Calvo. Held at the plantation house of Bernard de Marigny de Mandeville, facing the Mississippi River not far from today's Elysian Fields Avenue, the event started at 7 P.M. and continued until 7 A.M. the next morning.

Rooms in the mansion were ablaze with countless candles and oil lamps. The gaming tables that dotted the rooms were bustling. Several orchestras played dance music. There were twenty-four different types of gumbo—at least six contained sea turtle. Bavarian sweets covered the dessert tables. While many guests were seated for dinner, hundreds dined standing.

This was followed by yet another diplomatic ball on December 20. Tables were set up for games that included *ecarté*, *braque*, chess, *bête*, *médiateur*, *bouillotte*, and the then popular game of *creps*, better known in English as craps. There was more dancing, and a special sit-down supper was served at 1 A.M.

Artist John L. Boqueta de Woiseri's 1803 depiction of the city looks upriver from the Marigny plantation house and gardens, located near modern Elysian Fields Avenue and the Mississippi River. (The Historic New Orleans Collection)

An 1821 lithograph shows how the St. Louis Cathedral appeared in 1816. The church has long been a popular setting for Midnight Mass. (The Historic New Orleans Collection)

The City Council gave a ball the next day in honor of Madame Laussat. Her husband later wrote that at this ball, "the women had never been more elegant and fresh looking in their finery." In reference to all of the parties, he said, "Certainly the banks of the Mississippi had never before seen any gatherings or festivities so splendid and so lively."

Although the Creoles (the term then referring to locals mainly of French and Spanish descent) were not entirely pleased with their new American status, they did enjoy the festivities and participated in the dancing and celebrations. Controversy erupted, however, when it came to selection of dances not only at private parties, but also in the public dance halls. Some French sensitivities were offended when English dances, those familiar to Americans, were played in preference to French selections. Americans were equally put out when they thought too many French dances were being played. To Americans this was now their city. A compromise of sorts was reached when dances were alternated.

For a few years after the Louisiana Purchase, the start of the New Orleans Christmas season was observed beginning December 20, the day the city officially became part of the United States of America. Parades, parties, fireworks, and military exercises highlighted the anniversary.

The end of the holidays remained the traditional date of January 6, Epiphany or Twelfth Night, when Christianity decrees that the Magi or Three Wise Men visited the Christ child to present him with gifts of gold, frankincense, and myrrh.

The Invasion of the British

As celebratory and lighthearted as the Christmas season of 1803-4 was for the citizens of New Orleans, the holiday in 1814-15 was one of fear. The might of Great Britain was preparing to invade the city in the closing months of the War of 1812. Although a peace agreement had been signed at Ghent, in modern-day Belgium, news had not yet reached this side of the Atlantic. Few events would ever instill such concern in the city's residents. This anxiety might only be compared to the city's fall to Union forces during the Civil War in April 1862 or to the flooding and forced evacuation of New Orleans following Hurricane Katrina in 2005.

As early as the spring of 1814, word was spreading concerning an impending British attack on New Orleans and the Gulf Coast. By late November the British military buildup was beginning in Jamaica, and with word of this activity Maj. Gen. Andrew Jackson set out for New Orleans. He arrived on December 2. Eight days later a Jamaica-based British fleet of ten thousand troops anchored near Lake Borgne.

Jackson prepared New Orleans for imminent invasion. On December 22, British troops moved across the Gentilly plain toward the city, but in a surprise attack on the night of December 23, Jackson successfully stopped the enemy advance, prompting the invaders to move to the Chalmette plain along the Mississippi River and onto terrain more favorable for the American forces.

In December of 1814 prayers were said as usual in commemoration of the Nativity of the Christ child, but prayers asking that the city and its citizens be spared from British invaders quickly overshadowed these. On January 7, 1815—the day after Twelfth Night and the day before the Battle of New Orleans—the Ursuline nuns offered up such prayers to the Blessed Virgin Mary, also known as Our Lady of Prompt Succor. Their prayers were answered. On January 8, 1815, Jackson defeated the British with a resounding American victory at the Battle of New Orleans.

This pastel portrait of Andrew Jackson, the hero of the Battle of New Orleans, by Jean Baptiste Adolphe la Fosse dates from about 1840. (The Historic New Orleans Collection)

This romanticized and not entirely accurate view of the Battle of New Orleans dates from about 1860. Until the Civil War, Jackson's victory was commemorated on its January 8 anniversary with balls and parties that coincided with the end of the Christmas season in the New Orleans area. (The Historic New Orleans Collection)

For nearly half a century the Battle of New Orleans influenced the Christmas season. It no longer began on the December 20 anniversary of the Louisiana Purchase transfer but was shifted three days later to December 23, the anniversary of Jackson's first successful skirmish against Britain's forces. On December 23, 1816, the *Louisiana Gazette* commented on local patriotism saying, "the people of Louisiana first showed that they were willing to seal with their blood the compact that had already indissolubly bound them to the great American republic." While Twelfth Night remained the end of the religious celebration of Christmas in New Orleans, the close of the overall season was extended two extra days to January 8, the anniversary of the Battle of New Orleans.

For many years January 8 was a national holiday symbolizing American pride over having routed the British. In New Orleans a grand ball was held annually. But by the start of the Civil War in 1861 the balls no longer took place, and the city's unofficial end of the Christmas season shifted back to Twelfth Night, the sixth of January.

CHAPTER THREE

The 1800s through the 1900s

Beginning in the nineteenth century there was a movement among the middle classes in Europe and America to create a more pious, family-oriented Christmas season. The lives of middle-class children revolved around what was perceived as the "ideal childhood." They were dressed in proper clothes, played with proper toys, and went to the "correct" schools. Reflecting the middle classes' interest in cultivating childhood, Christmas grew into a children's holiday that revolved more around the family. As the American middle-class Christmas changed into something more genteel and refined—befitting middle-class tastes, ambitions, and sensibilities—so did Christmas in New Orleans.

Most of the changes took place during the period between 1820 and 1850. Holiday symbols such as cards, trees, and the tradition of Christmas shopping became part of the season. In the United States, *A Visit from St. Nicholas*—"'Twas the night before Christmas . . . "—credited to Clement C. Moore, was published in 1823. In England, Charles Dickens' *A Christmas Carol* debuted twenty years later to ultimately become a sensation on both sides of the Atlantic. Illustrated mass-circulation magazines such as the *Illustrated London News*, *Harper's Weekly*, and *Frank Leslie's Illustrated Newspaper* helped to further mold the modern Christmas, promoting family and giving. All of these were read in New Orleans.

In nineteenth-century New Orleans, for many Roman Catholic Creoles the ideal Christmas revolved around religion and family togetherness. It combined Victorian bourgeois attitudes with New Orleans Catholic traditions. There would have been no fireworks, noisemakers, or guns. It was a time to celebrate the birth of the Christ child and the family. Christmas Eve gatherings included grandparents, uncles, aunts, and of course children. Some families partook of a light meal before going to mass; others chose to fast. Sips of wine, eggnog, or cups of coffee would help keep locals awake as they waited to make the trek to Midnight Mass. As midnight drew near, Catholic families left home, some carrying lighted candles for the quiet procession through gaslit streets.

By 1850, St. Louis Cathedral had been rebuilt and the surrounding area beautified. The Pontalba apartment buildings were constructed in 1849-50; mansard roofs and cupolas were added to the Cabildo and

Presbytere. The ancient Place d'Armes was landscaped in the French style and modified to make room for a monument to Andrew Jackson. The equestrian statue, by Clark Mills, was dedicated in 1856, and the elegant square was renamed Jackson Square. (There is an identical statue in Lafayette Park in Washington, D.C.) The 1850s Cathedral structure that we know today would have been the same in which worshippers attended mass, except for some subsequent restorations and interior remodeling.

By the mid-nineteenth century there were many Midnight Masses held around town, as New Orleans had grown considerably. More Roman Catholic churches, such as St. Patrick's, St. Theresa of Avila, Immaculate Conception, St. Alphonsus, and St. Mary's Assumption, were constructed, yet Midnight Mass was not held in every church since holding the mass required permission from the archbishop. For many the Cathedral was the place to be, but there were now too many people residing in New Orleans for the venerable house of worship to hold everyone.

Creole families returned home after mass to enjoy a Christmas *réveillon*, or late-night meal, a French custom following the theater or some other evening event. (Translated *réveillon* means to "awaken").

The Place d'Armes was rechristened Jackson Square in honor of Andrew Jackson around 1850. At that time its gardens were beautified. The surrounding buildings, including the Pontalba Buildings, were newly constructed, and the Cabildo and Presbytere were remodeled with new roofs. The view has hardly changed since that time. (The Historic New Orleans Collection)

A Christmas *réveillon* was akin to a late-night breakfast and included such foods as eggs, sweetbreads, raisin bread, and the ever-popular *daube glacé*, a type of jellied meat. Also served were grillades (beef or veal round steak) and grits. For desserts there might be wine cakes and elaborately molded jellies, a popular Victorian treat, accompanied by wine and coffee. The *réveillon* became especially popular during the latter part of the nineteenth century and was a beloved part of the New Orleans Creole Christmas.

A popular place for a late-night meal after going to the French Opera House or a Carnival ball was the French Market, where partygoers would savor coffee. Although there were many restaurants open and crowded in New Orleans on Christmas Eve, for the more pious Catholic families a public place such as a restaurant was not considered appropriate to visit after Midnight Mass. They held their *réveillon* at home. Drinking and high jinks were also frowned upon; these were reserved for New Year's Eve.

For New Orleans Catholics, Christmas Day was a solemn one and a time for visiting family. Morning brought another breakfast for anyone who might still be hungry. Brioche with butter was served and of course more coffee. There were a few small presents in stockings for the children since the bigger, more lavish and expensive gifts were set aside for New Year's Day, a week later.

On Christmas morning family members took the younger children to the Cathedral and other churches to gaze in wonder at the *crèche,* or Nativity scene. On this day the churches were always packed. At each manger children offered a prayer to the Christ child.

In the decades following the Battle of New Orleans, New Orleans had grown dramatically. It was wealthy, influential, and the largest city in the South. By 1840 it had a population of over one hundred thousand and was the fourth-largest city in the nation. It vied with New York as the nation's leading banking center and greatest port. Germans, Irish, Italians, and many other nationalities brought their own Christmas celebrations to the Crescent City.

T. K. Wharton, a staunch Episcopalian who designed Christ Church, which stood on Canal at Dauphine Street between 1846 and 1885, always mentioned Christmas in his journal, but he made scant mention of attending church. In his household, the holiday was duly recognized and celebrated in an English manner: gifts for the children, walks, feasting, and even some work at home.

In 1854, Wharton wrote about how muggy the weather was leading up to Christmas. In such weather he found the celebration to be languid and spiritless. He preferred the "buoyant hilarity of the season in more rigorous latitudes." He sought a "quickener of the pulse of life in countries where winter is 'Winter.'"

O Christmas Tree!

By the start of the Civil War, Creole families in New Orleans were putting up Christmas trees of sorts along with their *crèches.* They also decorated with such holiday greenery as holly, mistletoe, and magnolia leaves, which were popular for Christmas in the South.

The decorated, candlelit Christmas fir tree was only a recent addition to the worldwide celebration of the holiday, but greenery had long been displayed during the winter solstice. Throughout Europe it was featured during mid-winter festivals. Holly, with its red berries symbolizing the blood of Christ and thorns representing the Crown of Thorns, along with ivy, had ancient wintertime roots. The Druids hung fruit on oak trees to honor their harvest gods, and as the *Daily Picayune* told its readers in 1859, "The idea of bedecking houses and churches with green boughs at Christmas time was Druidical, and has been used in Britain ever since the times of those ancient pagans. That custom still obtains with Christmas keepers in every country, our own included."

Tradition has it that the eighth-century missionary St. Boniface confronted German pagans by chopping down an oak tree at the German town of Geismar. He pointed at a fir tree, telling the pagans that the fir was a symbol people should revere since it is an evergreen and remains green throughout the coldest and bleakest months of the year.

A "paradise tree," among the forerunners of the Christmas tree, was used in medieval mystery plays to represent the Garden of Eden. Often a fir tree, paradise trees were erected in homes on Christmas Eve. Some paradise trees were decorated with apples or wafers symbolizing the Eucharist. In medieval Germany a custom grew of building pyramids of shelves with greenery and candles to symbolize a fir tree. Eventually the traditions of the pyramid and paradise tree were combined and used as a single Christmas decoration all over the Rhineland, part of the evolution of the decorated Christmas tree.

Evergreens were being sold in Germany for Christmas decorations as early as 1531, although it was not until the seventeenth century that decorated fir trees were displayed at Christmas in the homes of German Protestants. The decorated Christmas tree spread slowly from Protestant Germany to other parts of Europe, mostly via German royalty

In addition to small citrus trees, the wax myrtle was used by early New Orleanians as a Christmas tree. The setting for this photograph is the French Quarter's Hermann-Grima House, a house museum that depicts the way a prosperous family lived from the 1830s until 1860. (Courtesy Hermann-Grima Historic House)

marrying into other royal families. During the American Revolution, Hessian mercenaries in the employ of the British brought the Christmas tree to parts of the northeastern United States, as did German Protestant immigrants.

The Christmas tree was not reportedly seen in France until 1837 when Helen of Mecklenburg introduced the German tradition after her marriage to the Duc d'Orleans. The first popularization of the Christmas tree took place in the 1840s when British Queen Victoria's German-born husband, Prince Albert of Saxe-Coburg-Gotha, set up a Christmas tree at Windsor for his young family. In 1848 the *Illustrated London News,* one of the first mass-circulation magazines with a large worldwide readership, ran an engraved image of the family standing around a decorated tabletop tree. Almost immediately well-to-do families in England and America followed suit. The first American tree lot was established in New York City in 1851, and five years later the White House trimmed its first Christmas tree.

During the 1840s, as more German immigrants settled in New Orleans, they were among the first people in the Crescent City to put up decorated Christmas trees. In an 1886 article in the *Daily Picayune* it was stated that the *Deutscher Turn Verein,* German Turners' Association (a men's gymnastic society that promoted athletic and cultural activities), had been putting up a tree since the group was founded, during the waves of the German immigrants' arrival in the Crescent City some forty years earlier.

One of the earliest public displays of a decorated Christmas fir tree in New Orleans was in 1855, when the ladies of St. Paul's Episcopal Church placed a decorated fir tree in the Masonic Hall at the corner of St. Charles and Perdido Streets. Those who came to see the tree were expected to make a donation to help raise funds for completion of the interior of the congregation's new church on Camp Street near Coliseum Place. According to the *Daily Picayune,* "Setting up of Christmas trees was a German custom of late years imported into the United States to the great delight of young folk." Of the St. Paul's display, the newspaper described "a tree of evergreen . . . hung with brilliant lights and laden with Christmas gifts, delicacies, ornaments, etc." It also "attracted a good deal of attention."

On December 24, 1855, T. K. Wharton wrote that his wife had "astounded" the children on that dark and gloomy Christmas Eve with "a tasteful 'Christmas Tree' all hung with Christmas presents and garnished around with fruits and a variety of pretty objects. . . . Tommy [his son] was amazed and delighted beyond measure, and Ellen [his daughter] only wished that Christmas Eve could be protracted to an indefinite duration."

When fir trees were not available, substitutes were freely used. This was especially true in New Orleans before the 1880s. Wharton did not mention the type of tree displayed in his home, but it can be assumed that his was not a fir. On Christmas Eve, 1856, he wrote of going to market in the morning to buy the family's Christmas dinner and while there met up with an office assistant named Mr. Keen. Mr. Keen was loaded down with boughs of wild orange covered with fruit, myrtle orange, and arbor vitae (a type of cone-bearing evergreen similar to a cedar) for the Wharton family Christmas tree. Wharton's son was in "ecstasies" with the tree, which was decorated with presents and fruit showing through the branches.

Eliza Ripley, in her 1912 memoir *Social Life in Old New Orleans*, recalls her Christmas of 1859 spent at an upriver plantation. "Boys," she wrote, "were ransacking the distant woods for holly branches and magnolia boughs," all traditional southern holiday greenery. "We had a tree," she added. "None of us had ever seen a Christmas tree; there were no cedars or pines, so we finally settled upon a tall althea bush, hung presents on it, for all the house servants, as well as for the family and a few guests. The tree had to be lighted up, so it was postponed until evening."

For several years S. N. Moody, wealthy owner of a successful men's haberdashery on Canal Street, put up a Christmas tree for his children and their playmates. The children all came in costume and played around the "treasure laden branches." In 1866 the *Daily Picayune* reported on the splendid sixteen-foot Japanese plum tree that stood under the arch separating two large parlors in the Moody home.

Trees were decorated not only with presents, but fruit, flowers, and even Spanish moss. By the 1860s glass ornaments from Germany became available. In 1877 an Uptown New Orleans schoolgirl named

By the mid-1880s, when this photograph was taken at the Maier and Engelbach family gathering, fir Christmas trees hung with presents had become commonplace in New Orleans during the holidays. (The Historic New Orleans Collection)

By the early twentieth century Christmas had evolved primarily into a children's holiday, and whether their presents were delivered by an all-American Santa Claus or a Creole Pere Noël, children all over New Orleans looked with equal awe and excitement at the gift-laden family Christmas tree. (The Historic New Orleans Collection)

Victoria Raymond wrote to a friend about her Sunday school Christmas tree: "You must not disappoint me by failing to come to witness the Christmas tree." she said. The next year she recalled that the Sunday school tree was dressed "with the usual evergreens and flowers."

By the 1880s fir trees were beginning to show up regularly in New Orleans, especially in public buildings and institutions. In 1884, for instance, the children of St. Vincent's Infant Asylum were treated to a tree that reached the ceiling and touched the surrounding walls. Two years later the *Daily Picayune* reported that the German Turners' Association "regaled the little ones with a grand Christmas tree and presentation of gifts . . . The magnificent Christmas tree laden with chosen gifts and sweetmeats and fruits of every description was placed in the middle of the spacious Washington Artillery Hall, on St. Charles. . . . The happy little ones danced around [it] until 10 o'clock."

Most families at the time did not have such large room-filling trees, but throughout the 1880s more and larger fir trees were becoming available as tree farms sprang up across the country and local

By 1914, when this photograph was taken, a fir Christmas tree was a fixture of the holiday in New Orleans and throughout the United States. (The Historic New Orleans Collection)

nurseries and florists began to stock them. In 1890 one such New Orleans retailer was R. Maitre, florist and seed man on Canal Street near Carondelet. He advertised, "Spruce Pine/I offer them in sizes and prices so everybody is enabled to enjoy their own Xmas Tree!" In 1904 the *Daily Picayune* reported, "Christmas trees twinkling with lights were to be seen through windows of mansions and cottages all over the city."

In 1904 candles on trees were the norm. Nostalgic twentieth-century recollections of Creole Christmases often point out how children marveled at the sight of the candlelit tree on Christmas morning, which was the only time it would be lit, as was the case in most of America, because it was a fire hazard. Buckets of water were always kept nearby.

Electric tree lights appeared in the 1880s, but at first their use was very limited. However, in the early twentieth century the New Orleans Electric Light Company was promoting them despite the fact that few homes had electricity until the 1920s.

Christmas Gifts

The custom of giving Christmas gifts is as old as the Magi presenting their gifts to the Christ child. During the nineteenth century the custom blossomed as never before with the growing commercialization and evolution of Christmas as a children's holiday. Among the Creoles of New Orleans small trifles were given on Christmas Day, but they were in no way meant to overshadow the religious solemnity of the holy day. The more expensive gifts were saved for New Year's Day. Youngsters would return from visits to relatives with arms loaded down with presents. Whether one received their gifts on Christmas, more the norm for the city's growing American population, or on New Year's Day, the purchase of presents had already emerged as one of the most important parts of the season.

This Daily Picayune *ad from the early 1900s urged locals to shop early. The frog was a longtime symbol of the publication. (The Historic New Orleans Collection)*

The *Southern Traveler*, a newspaper from the former City of Lafayette, now the Garden District and Irish Channel, said in an editorial on December 24, 1843, "how in anticipation, in laughing, budding childhood, we could see 'the Old Belsnickle' [in Germany one of the gift giver's helpers who quizzed children on their behavior] stealing . . . to our bedside, to deposit his store of good things . . . [now] we might examine our stock of presents;—how neatly our new trowsers [*sic*] fit; how brilliantly shine the buttons on our new jacket." In this neighborhood of mostly newly arrived Anglo-Americans and German and Irish immigrants, the chief gifts came out on Christmas Day and not New Year's.

The Americans and Creoles did have something in common when the writer in the *Southern Traveler* wrote "how . . . father stirred *that* bowl of 'egg nogg.'" Eggnog was a favorite holiday drink for both French and Americans. Of French origin, *lait de poule* was made of eggs, milk, and spices. When the English-speaking world discovered it, they added liquor and nutmeg and called it "nog," an old English word for ale.

By the 1850s the promotion of Christmas goods and their display was becoming increasingly bigger business. In 1854, T. K. Wharton described how the stores on Chartres and Royal Streets were decked out with their "splendid" displays of Christmas and New Year's novelties.

The Anglo Whartons exchanged their gifts on Christmas morning; Wharton never mentioned a New Year's or Twelfth Night gift. Wharton enjoyed recounting in his journal the array of gifts under the tree for his children, such as the Mazarin blue cloak he and his wife gave his son in 1853 and a fireman's hat a few years later. He commented on the admirable dressing gown he himself received in 1859.

The economy in New Orleans was especially good in New Orleans in 1859, and it manifested itself in a memorably lavish and big spending Christmas. On December 25, the *Daily Picayune* described the "tempting profusion of riches" in the city's show windows, and some items reached what was then the princely sum of two thousand dollars. "The appearance of our variety stores," said the *Picayune*, "has been more brilliant this year than we have ever known them to be. . . . These tempting bazaars are crowded all day and until a late hour of the night by ladies and children, and a goodly number of the sterner set, who are performing the solemn duty of buying Christmas gifts."

On Christmas Day, 1859, the *Daily Picayune* was in a "somewhat voluminous shape" with its first sixteen-page issue. The newspaper had experienced a steady and large increase in its advertisers. This was obvious in the pages of advertising in the issue, and the *Picayune* took the opportunity to extend to its patrons, "one and all, a right merry Christmas, and many joyful returns of the day."

Christmas cards were fairly new to the United States in the 1880s. Printed cards first appeared in England in 1843. In 1870, German-born lithographer Louis Prang, residing in the United States, began exporting elegant, artistic Christmas cards to England, where they were instantly successful. By 1890, Prang was selling over five million cards annually to Americans; at the same time inexpensive cards were beginning to appear, soon driving Prang out of the Christmas card business.

Au Bon Marche on Canal Street sold "Prang's and other Christmas Cards and novelties." In 1884 this store had some of the most ambitious holiday advertising in New Orleans when across three columns of the *Daily Picayune* the store proclaimed that it "Wishes A Merry X-MAS to All." It highlighted the store's numerous Christmas goodies such as fans, gloves, and jewelry, along with "Thousands of . . . fine dolls in Wax and Biscuit from 25¢ to $35 apiece." What a lucky little girl to receive a $35 doll in the 1880s!

With the end of the nineteenth century, Christmas advertisements in New Orleans newspapers became still larger and more ambitious in their design. Modern store advertising had come of age as large illustrated ads covered full pages. In 1895 an S. J. Shwartz ad filling almost an entire newspaper page had columns of "Christmas Bargains." D. H. Holmes department store touted itself "The Store of the Christmas Spirit." In 1889, S. Kuhn & Son pondered the season: "The Advent of our Glorious Holiday. Merry Christmas with its pleasant anticipations, golden opportunities, and delightful realities will soon be here . . . . Yet perplexities as well. What Shall I Get For Others?" An answer was provided by Kreeger's, the upscale women's shop. For those with little girls, Kreeger's answer was, "DOLLS! This is the season of Dolls, and we are in full array with thousands of lovely dolls."

By the end of the nineteenth century New Year's gifts seem to have been losing their allure and the Anglo-American tradition of Christmas Day gifts was infiltrating New Orleans' Creole families since stores were no longer advertising anything for the New Year.

Here Comes Santa Claus

Along with the growth of gift giving and the evolution of department store Christmas advertising, there came the jolly elfin gift giver, Santa Claus. Santa is an American invention that came to dominate the secular side of worldwide Christmas.

Santa Claus has a long lineage of gift-giving ancestors across Europe and the Americas. Most notably there was St. Nicholas of Myra, a fourth-century bishop beloved for his kindness to children. By the twelfth century he was the patron saint of children and gifts were given on his feast day, December 6. With the Protestant Reformation in the sixteenth century, St. Nicholas fell out of favor in such Protestant countries as Germany, where other gift givers took over, including the Christ child and Kris Kringle.

In Puritan England, Scotland, and the northeastern United States, gift giving faded as the celebration of Christmas fell from grace. Following the French Revolution and its disregard for organized religion, Christmas went into abeyance in France. However, the Dutch retained a love of Christmas and a gift giver named Sinter Klass.

In early-nineteenth-century New York a group of writers, including James Fenimore Cooper, Washington Irving, and Clement C. Moore—reputed author of *A Visit from St. Nicholas*, first published in 1823—formed a group called the Knickerbockers, a name derived from Irving's *Knickerbocker's History of New York*. They created a distinctly American Christmas celebration that was neither British nor Catholic and invented Santa Claus, claiming that he was based on Sinter Klass, for whom early Dutch New Yorkers had great affection. This image was a bit far fetched since there is no evidence of any adherence to Sinter Klass in early New York, but the Knickerbockers' vision of a jolly gift giver riding through the sky, jumping down chimneys, and putting gifts in stockings became an instant hit with children. New York merchants saw Santa as a way to increase often sluggish year-end sales. Moore's poem, published anonymously in

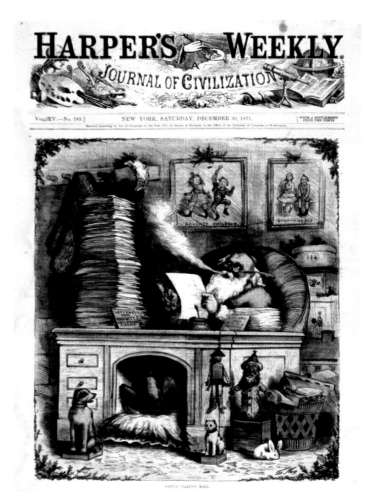

By 1871, when this drawing of Santa Claus by Thomas Nast appeared in Harper's Weekly, *children throughout America, including New Orleans, sent letters to Santa asking for Christmas presents. It was Nast who helped create the look and demeanor of the Santa much of the world accepts today. (The Historic New Orleans Collection)*

a Troy, New York, newspaper, would add the cast of eight tiny reindeer along with their names: "Now, DASHER! now, DANCER! now, PRANCER and VIXEN!/On, COMET! on CUPID! on DONDER and BLITZEN!"

The story of Santa and his reindeer spread beyond New York and was quickly embraced by children who fell in love with the happy elf who was nothing like a stiff bishop of old. Santa became part of the middle-class family-oriented Christmas celebration.

"HELLO! LITTLE ONE!"

Here Santa Claus is depicted to be as modern as the age he is in, and in 1884, Harper's Weekly *artist Thomas Nast had Santa taking a request from a child over a newfangled telephone rather than by letter. (The Historic New Orleans Collection)*

By 1859, Santa was already in New Orleans, and that year the *Daily Picayune* printed "For The Young Folks" a poem titled "Santa Claus's Visit," which partly reads:

Awake dear mamma! And do
    come and see
What Santa Claus left in my
    stocking for me:
I've a doll and a sofa, and many
    fine things.
What beautiful presents old
    Santa Claus brings! . . .
Oh *dear*! Don't you think, when
    I'm older next year,
I can keep *wide awake* to see the
    reindeer?

Santa took on various guises until he became the stout, bearded, red-coat-clad gentleman we know today. This popularly accepted image grew out of the imagination of German-born Thomas Nast, a political cartoonist for *Harper's Weekly* from the 1860s through the 1880s. With that magazine's huge circulation, Santa's image was quickly recognized and embraced across America.

Nast had a decidedly Union bias and during the Civil War his Santa Claus cared about the well-being of Northern troops and their families. Throughout Reconstruction, Nast's attitudes continued to be highly anti-Southern, although he could be just as critical of Northern politicians. His cartoons were especially vicious towards Louisiana and New Orleans during those violent days of Reconstruction. From Nast's cartoons it would seem that Santa Claus had deserted Southern children. In 1867 the book *General Lee and Santa Claus*, written by Louise Clack, explained that Santa had not actually deserted the children of the Confederacy, but rather, at the request of Gen. Robert E. Lee himself, had joined the Southern effort by helping to care for their own wounded fathers and brothers.

No matter what, by 1866, Santa Claus was still in the good graces of New Orleans youngsters, and he was influencing Christmas in New Orleans as much as in every other part of the United States. In spite of Thomas Nast's Northern leanings, Santa was indeed as Southern as he was anything else. In 1866 the Grand Bazaar, B. Piffet in the Touro block on Canal Street, advertised itself as "Old Santa Claus's Headquarters," where there were "TOYS TOYS TOYS from London, Paris, Vienna, Leipzig." Santa Claus at Piffet's also stocked "Rich, Fancy and Useful Artifacts From all parts of the Known World." While Piffet may have advertised using an American Santa Claus, he conceded to the New Orleans Creole custom of advertising both Christmas and New Year's holiday presents. The same year Guéblé & Nippert had "Christmas Presents For All . . . the most magnificent display of Holiday Goods ever brought within the reach of Santa Claus," while the *Daily Picayune,* in describing a large Christmas tree in 1866, said that it "gave simple testimony to the genius and taste of Santa Claus, the never failing friend of all good children."

By the 1880s virtually every large store on Canal Street had its own Santa Claus, which must have necessitated some explaining by parents to their confused kids. Santa was even promoting presents for father. In 1895, H. B. Stevens & Co., the elegant Canal Street men's store, went all out with an early illustrated advertisement showing Santa sliding down a chimney with his sack of presents from Stevens with the caption "Santa Claus Has Been Busy."

In 1877, New Orleans schoolgirl Victoria Raymond wrote that at her Sunday school Christmas party she knew "who is going to be Santa Claus and also, some of the gifts to be distributed." Of the Sunday school party in 1878 she wrote in detail about some of the tableaux presented, and with a bit of imagination wrote that "after some of the tableaux Santa Claus came in his chariot drawn by six reindeer. His tree near loaded with gifts." Raymond concluded, "All [were] contented with our gifts & returned home charmed & sorry it had come so soon to a close."

Santa Claus became indelibly etched in the minds of virtually all American children, and by the end of the nineteenth century, he was the omnipresent figure of secular American Christmas. In 1895, two years before little Virginia O'Hanlon asked the editor of the *New York Sun* if there was a Santa Claus, prompting the immortal answer, "Yes, Virginia, there is a Santa Claus," the editors of the *Daily Picayune* in New Orleans wrote in a similar manner. "Keep up the illusion," wrote the paper. "Speaking of Santa Claus, it seems like down right cruelty . . . to . . . dissipate the illusions . . . concerning Santa Claus . . . let us all believe in our St. Nicks as long as possible." The *Daily Picayune*'s Santa editorial may now be mostly forgotten; however, William B. Reily & Company of New Orleans has for many years

England's Father Christmas, as shown in the Illustrated Weekly London News *in 1855, was not a children's gift giver like America's Santa Claus, but rather promoted feasting, drinking, and merriment, which was how many New Orleanians celebrated Christmas. (The Historic New Orleans Collection)*

paid for the reprinting of the *New York Sun* editorial in the *New Orleans Times-Picayune* on Christmas Day.

The American Santa Claus was different from Britain's traditional Father Christmas, who represented adult merriment, eating, and drinking and did not even bring gifts to children until the late nineteenth century as the popularity of Santa encouraged British merchants to turn Father Christmas into a more jovial children's gift giver. Pere Noël in his similarity to Santa Claus became a middle-class, nineteenth-century stand-in for France's le Petit Jésus or le Petit Noël, a gift giver representing the baby Jesus.

In 1870 the Canal Street store Guéblé & Nippert called itself "Santa's headquarters" in English-language newspapers, and in the French-language newspaper *L'Abeille de la Nouvelle Orleans*, also known as *The Bee*, the store advertised, "Cadeaux De Noel!" Lion & Pinsard, another Canal Street store, advertised, "Noël! Noël!! Et Jour De L'An" but no mention of Santa.

In 1898, *The Bee* ran a political cartoon showing Uncle Sam filling the stockings of the newly acquired territories, the Philippines, Puerto Rico, Hawaii, and Cuba, with the caption, *"Oncle Sam Comme Papa Noël/Remplissant les bas ses enfants adoptifs."* [Uncle Sam as Papa Noël filling the stockings of his adopted children.] For many Creole kiddies it was indeed Papa Noël who filled their stockings with trinkets on Christmas morning. An illustration in the same 1898 issue depicts an unnamed white-bearded gift bringer of military bearing wearing an ermine-lined cap and jacket, buttoned leggings, and carrying a sword. He is astride a single reindeer.

A charming cartoon in *The Bee* of Christmas 1901 has the caption "Bonhomme Noël Fait Des Heureux." [Good Man Christmas Makes Them Happy.] It shows a jolly Santa-like elfin man frolicking with two children. In an accompanying poem he is called *"le viellard,"* the old man.

Whether they called him Papa Noël or the "old man," as the nineteenth century drew to a close the children of French New Orleans had adopted today's more familiar gift giver, an American Santa Claus.

Santa dances with a fashionable lady on the cover of the December 15, 1930, New Orleanian *magazine. (The Historic New Orleans Collection)*

Instead of using reindeer for transportation, Santa has opted for a donkey on the cover of the December 1931 New Orleanian. *(The Historic New Orleans Collection)*

Early Christmas Fireworks

Throughout the nineteenth century, with the beginning of the Christmas season came a disruptive boom: blasts of fireworks that lasted until New Year's or even Twelfth Night. Fireworks had been a part of Christmas in New Orleans since the city was a colony, but demonstrations of yuletide noise weren't unique to its inhabitants. Fire, firecrackers, ringing bells, snapping whips, loud horns—indeed any loud noises and bright light—were common virtually everywhere in the Christian world at Christmastime. Blasting guns and rifles into the air was also popular at Christmas, especially in the South. The making of racket grew out of the belief that demonic forces were driven off only by noise. Around the turn of the nineteenth century, there were several impressive fireworks displays in conjunction with the Louisiana Purchase transfer festivities and the victory at the Battle of New Orleans. These public displays succeeded in fueling the continuation of such Christmas activities by individuals. Residents had always been quick to shoot off a firecracker or two during the holidays and began to stock up in ever-increasing amounts.

In 1853, English-born and Ohio-reared Thomas K. Wharton was

the superintendent in charge of the construction of the United States Custom House in New Orleans. He wrote in his diary on December 23 that there was "a good deal of firing and other demonstrations" in honor of the events leading up to the January 8 victory at Chalmette.

The "sounds" of the season began in the middle of December and were especially loud on Christmas Eve and again on New Year's Eve. T. K. Wharton wrote in 1854 that on Christmas Day his children made a "lively uproar" with firecrackers from morning until night. Fireworks were readily available in all types of shops, and even children were able to purchase gunpowder. In 1859, B. Piffet, an upscale Canal Street dry goods dealer, advertised, "Fireworks. Rockets. Roman Candles. Revolving Wheels. Flower Pots. Torpedoes. &c. &c. &c." The candy manufacturer Norman & Reiss on Old Levee (Decatur) Street in 1870 offered for sale a long list of "Fire Works" such as flying pigeons, serpents, torpedoes, tourbillions, and various wheels, along with candies, pastas, and Christmas gifts.

On December 27, 1859, the *Daily Picayune* reported that a man dressed in a combination of military and civilian clothing was beating on a drum while he walked the streets with a band of urchins in tow. He was supposedly crazed by the incessant and continual noise that filled the city. On January 6, 1860, the paper reported that the horrendous noise emanating from the "explosion of crackers, fireworks and firearms" had driven another man insane. The sounds made horses and mules difficult to handle, and many animals tried to run away with each blast. Some people questioned why the city during such a religious season devoted itself to so much mirth, fun, frolic, and noise.

The Civil War

On December 20, 1860, South Carolina seceded from the Union, and people in New Orleans knew that war was imminent. Such concerns, however, did not stop the usual fireworks and holiday cheer. On December 26 the *Daily Picayune* commented that "Christmas Eve and Christmas Day were duly celebrated with much burning of powder and draining of liquor bottles" and that "quiet folks, nervous old ladies and peevish old gentlemen were startled from their sleep, kept in a state of continual trepidation and alarm, and made most miserable by the explosions of fire crackers, pistols, guns and in fact all the noisy engines invented by a tormenting genius."

The following year Louisiana seceded. The nation was at war with itself and by Christmas, Federal troops began assembling at Ship Island off the Mississippi Gulf coast. During the holiday season, the fear of Union attack circulated around New Orleans, producing much the same anxiety as the British attack at Christmas 1814. In 1861 there was now concern as to whether New Orleans could be successfully defended.

In spite of impending doom and possible economic collapse, Christmas went on as usual in the Crescent City. The *Daily Picayune* on December 25 said, "Let everyone be jolly," adding optimistically that it "had not seen our streets so gay as they were last night" in quite some time. Shops were filled with people buying Christmas gifts, although the *Picayune* found that the less expensive gifts were in greater demand than usual.

Not concerned about finances at this point, T. K. Wharton took his children to buy presents on Christmas Eve. The family put up an evergreen Christmas tree decorated with fruit and under it was an assortment of gifts that included such luxuries as jewelry, silver, drawings, and a set of tools for son Tommy. Wharton spent between two hundred and three hundred dollars and paid cash. This was a fairly large sum for a family of modest means to spend in wartime, but Wharton felt that with the stagnant economy it was one's duty to spend dollars more freely.

There were the usual fireworks, crackers, and pistol shots, and Wharton wrote that Tommy was "noisier than usual having invested extensively in fire crackers, and 'detonators.'"

The *Daily Picayune* found that the city was celebrating as best it could: "The Germans spent a great portion of the night singing their dearest *Weihnachtslieder*, and the French, sitting around the festive board, did their best to have as lively a *réveillon* as it is possible."

The city fell to the Union in April 1862. With the Federal naval blockade dropped, the port immediately reopened. After experiencing economic collapse and near starvation, the city's economy spun back into motion.

During the Christmas of 1863 street urchins were shooting off fireworks as usual while shop windows were filled with displays of toys and dolls and expensive items, including jewels. The *New Orleans Times* reported that wealthy ladies of fashion who were making their purchases for the holidays were visiting Canal, Chartres, and Royal Streets. The war, which was still raging, was never far from anyone's thoughts, and the *Times* hoped that some of the elegant ladies in the shops would assist children made orphans by the conflict.

With the end of hostilities in 1865, Christmas was celebrated with considerable gaiety and abandon. The streets of New Orleans overflowed with elegantly dressed shoppers. Canal Street, by then overtaking Chartres and Royal Streets as the city's center of elegant retail trade, was noticeably busy. The more pious made their way to church services, while others filled the theaters and restaurants, attended private parties, or visited friends and family. Locals served Christmas eggnog in copious amounts and the ever-present loud cackle of fireworks filled the ears.

Dangers of the Season

Along with all the fireworks there was gunfire, making Christmas Eve in the Crescent City not only joyous, but also dangerous. Newspapers were somewhat glib when they reported the fireworks and gunfire casualties of the season. They treated the accidents as if they were just part of the scene and were not responded to with the negative feeling that would build in later years

Throughout the late nineteenth and early twentieth centuries there were incidents of firecrackers setting buildings on fire. There were also accounts of fireworks thrown through open windows, causing fires or injury. In the 1880s a family was surprised during Christmas dinner when a bullet came through an open window and landed on their dining table. Most Christmas injuries were fortunately minor, and although the police condemned the use of guns and fireworks, nothing much was done to stop it until the twentieth century.

On Christmas Day, 1910, the *Daily Picayune* noted, "Christmas time is always a busy time at Charity Hospital, because fire-works and bad whiskey make victims for the surgeon's knife." The hospital reported that the number of fireworks injuries was down from previous years, "but the number of gunshot wounds was much larger." At the time most of the gunshot wounds were among the black community, "who were especially fond of celebrating Christmas with gunfire," according to the *Picayune*. Indeed, as a child New Orleans-born jazz legend Louis Armstrong was arrested for shooting a gun into the air on New Year's Eve. He was arrested and placed in the Colored Waifs Home for Boys for a period that Armstrong later reflected was a turning point in his life.

Church Services

In 1884 the *Daily Picayune* found "much to be regretted" about Christmas Eve since "the celebration had also its rowdy and disgraceful side. Egg Nog and its less dainty and more violent kindred were abroad in copious quantities. The spirit of riotous mischief was developed and showed itself before the night was out. It was no respecter of the ears or sensibilities of others and made itself obnoxious in every way." The *Picayune* bemoaned, "The horn-blowing hoodlum had destroyed the beautiful purpose of Christmas observations."

The secular side of Christmas was growing rapidly throughout the nineteenth century and fears concerning the loss of the true meaning of Christmas were as prevalent as today. However, the noise of gunfire and firecrackers could not drown out the bells from the city's many churches that rang from before midnight on Christmas Eve until the middle of Christmas Day. Even at the height of the revels on Canal Street, many people in the overwhelmingly Catholic city began breaking away from the crowds as church bells began to ring out for Midnight Mass.

For a pious Creole family attendance at Midnight Mass was regarded as obligatory, but no longer was St. Louis Cathedral the only house of prayer. In the 1870s the grandest and most solemn Midnight Mass was at St. Anne's Church in the Treme neighborhood. So popular was the mass there that every seat was generally filled well before midnight. In 1875 the *Daily Picayune* reported that the church held the "respectability of our Creole population."

One of the most impressive midnight Christmas celebrations was held at St. Anna's Episcopal Church, then located on Esplanade Avenue at Royal Street. To prevent crowding, the church doors opened at 11 P.M. and were closed to further admittance at midnight. People of all faiths visited St. Anna's. Indeed the city's Episcopal churches, such as St. Anna's, Christ Church, and Trinity, made extra Christmas preparations to provide some of the finest Christmas music in the city.

Churches that did not celebrate Midnight Mass opened their doors at the first light of dawn, some at 4 A.M., and masses were celebrated in every church throughout the day. For Catholic children much of Christmas Day was spent visiting as many churches as possible to see the crèches, also called the "stable" or "crib." Non-Catholics would also visit. Some crèches were lavish and beautifully arranged among palm fronds, flowers, and seasonal greens. In 1875, for instance, the *Daily Picayune* reported that the "crib" at St. Patrick's was "resplendent in the glories of a thousand candles."

Choirs sang throughout the day on Christmas. Catholic churches were packed from dawn to dusk. In the Church of the Immaculate Conception (today referred to as "Jesuit") on Baronne Street in downtown New Orleans, one of the city's largest and loveliest houses of worship, there were crowds all day long. The city's major Catholic houses of worship provided music programs featuring some of the city's finest performers.

These Christmas programs were outlined in detail in the newspapers the next day. Often entire sermons were summarized, such as one sermon given at Christ Church in 1895 concerning the appropriateness of the use of the term "mass" in the Episcopal Church.

Virtually every church in town was elaborately decorated with greenery and lights befitting the season. In 1886, the newly constructed Grace Episcopal Church was described as having beautiful and tasteful decorations. In 1895, St. Paul's Lutheran Church on Port at Burgundy Street erected a large Christmas tree with presents below its branches for children after the service, which was delivered in German. The same year St. Paul's Episcopal on Camp Street near Coliseum Place was decorated with cypress twigs that were woven together to form garlands around the church's pillars. The church was green throughout, and the entwined greenery was described as looking as if it went on forever.

The year 1880 was an especially good one for local church Christmas decorations. This was a reflection of the city's improved economy following the end of Reconstruction in 1877. Indeed, it was said then that the churches looked grander than they had in years. Several Christmas sermons referred to New Orleans' brilliant economic future.

In the St. Louis Cathedral that year there were masses of artificial (probably silk and wax) flowers covering the altars that were brilliantly illuminated by candles and gas jets. At St. Patrick's there was a profusion of real flowers, and hundreds of flickering candles provided some illumination at the altar and the crib.

Just as Canal Street and its stores were transformed by electric lights, this invention also transformed the Christmas decorations in churches, perhaps encouraging increased attendance. In 1895, Christ Church, which was decorated with palms and evergreens, featured a gigantic Star of Bethlehem made of incandescent light bulbs hung high above the altar. In 1904 the Church of the Immaculate Conception, once called the "church of candles," was adorned with white roses, calla lilies, and maidenhair fern; a welcome addition to its vast interior and golden bronze altar was the glow of hundreds of electric light bulbs.

Christmas Day Shopping and Dining

While many New Orleanians poured into churches for a bit of solemnity, on Christmas Day street revelers regrouped for yet another assault. Fireworks, horns, and drums renewed their sounds, which had barely died down from the night before. The streets were again packed; New Orleans wasn't entirely pious on Christmas Day.

While the Creole family may have frowned on a Christmas *réveillon* held outside the home, some New Orleanians were more than happy to go out for their feast. Restaurants and hotel dining rooms made themselves available on Christmas Eve and Christmas Day with menus that were especially fancy. Through the late nineteenth century many stores were open for business as the shopping rush continued. Theaters were open with Christmas Day matinees dedicated to and patronized by ladies and children, the latter clutching brand-new toys. Another popular retreat on Christmas Day was the Fair Grounds race track.

With thousands of people converging on Canal Street to attend church and places of entertainment, the city's numerous streetcar companies extended their service during both Christmas Eve and Christmas Day. Some lines added extra cars and ran as often as every ten minutes. As a result, the drivers and conductors had to work extra long and busy hours. As holiday compensation, the railway companies joined forces to provide a big, festive luncheon for company employees. In 1895, the luncheon was held at both Tranchina's and Olivieri's Restaurants. In all, more than eight hundred men enjoyed themselves at a feast that included after-dinner cigars.

Another favorite place for New Orleanians to visit on Christmas, especially after church services, was the public markets, most notably the French Market, which could be very crowded. Here they bought Christmas dinner, usually turkeys. In 1886 the *Daily Picayune* reported that "there were turkeys without number, the usages of the day compelling the slaughter of the crowned lords of the festive board." Seasonal produce such as apples and oranges were stacked high; also available were fresh breads and decorated Christmas cakes. The French Market was adorned throughout with countless bunches of flowers, garlands of greenery, and Christmas trees for purchase. In 1900 the stall keepers boasted displays that included Spanish moss, holly, palms, flowers, and flags.

Santa Claus Visits the World's Fair, 1884

By the late 1850s, the popularity of Santa Claus as the deliverer of

Frank Leslie's Illustrated Newspaper *depicts the enormous tree that was on display in the Music Hall of the Main Building on Christmas Day, 1884, at the World's Industrial and Cotton Centennial Exposition. Every child who attended the fair that day received a present. (From the collection of Peggy Scott Laborde)*

gifts had already taken hold in the United States. One of New Orleans' most memorable public visits from Santa Claus occurred on Christmas Day, 1884, at the World's Industrial and Cotton Centennial Exposition. The World's Fair opened on December 17, 1884, in the Upper City (Audubon) Park. On Christmas Day bells chimed at 6 A.M. The gates opened early and children were admitted half-price. A Christmas concert was held in the Music Hall and twenty black students from Leland University sang carols at the Colored Department fair exhibit.

At 5 P.M. all of the children were invited to meet Santa Claus to receive a Christmas toy. The event took place in the great Music Hall that seated eight thousand inside the mammoth Main Building. The

Frank Leslie's Illustrated Newspaper *shows Santa Claus at the 1884 World's Industrial and Cotton Centennial Exposition in New Orleans. Lacking the traditional Santa garb, this Santa borrowed clothing from an explorer in the Arctic Exhibit. He is shown distributing gifts in front of a giant Christmas tree that was among the earliest in New Orleans to be lit by electric lights. (The Historic New Orleans Collection)*

site of the building encompassed most of today's Audubon Park Golf Course. Thomas K. Pickering, the fair commissioner representing Connecticut, played Santa. He had a bit of a problem though—there was no Santa costume. Commissioner Pickering ultimately borrowed an explorer's outfit from the Arctic Exhibit. The costume, a full-length coat of reindeer fur with a boa of Siberian sable, didn't exactly resemble Santa's traditional garb. The tall boots were made of sealskin lined with wool and sea lion fur. But this backup garb worked.

By this time fir trees were commonplace at public Christmas events— and the bigger the better. A forty-five-foot-tall tree was shipped to the fair from a farm near New Haven, Connecticut. Its enormous branches were covered with large decorations. Seven thousand wrapped gifts circled the tree in anticipation of the expected throng of youngsters. No child went away empty handed.

At 6 P.M., while toys were being given out as the chilly, rainy day moved closer to dusk, six massive steam dynamos were set into motion. The fair's system of incandescent lights was switched on for the first time. All at once electric lights blazed in the huge hall. Around the hall and over the towering Christmas tree dangled clusters of electric lights draped to look like bunches of morning glory vines. They cast a warm glow throughout the great vaulted room. "The hall was resplendent," declared the *Daily Picayune*, "with rays of hundreds of Edison's incandescent electric lights."

Some of New Orleans' major streets were already lined with electric streetlights, but the incandescent bulb was only a few years old and most people would not yet have seen them in such profusion. This was one of the largest uses of electric lighting to date and every major building was outlined with strings of glowing bulbs. The fair became a wonderland of twinkling lights.

Horticultural Hall, a giant six-hundred-foot-long greenhouse filled with tropical flowering plants, stood where part of the Audubon Zoo is today. The hall was not only outlined in lights, but also crowned with a giant spotlight. Inside lights shone through the multitude of plate-glass windows.

Electricity added to the growing magic of Christmas. Introduced to New Orleans in 1882, tall electric lights were installed along the Mississippi riverfront. Over the next few years, electric streetlights were installed along Canal Street to its terminus at the cemeteries and along St. Charles Avenue all the way to Audubon Park. By the late 1920s most homes had electricity.

The Season Changes

It wasn't until the early twentieth century that Thanksgiving marked the "official" beginning of the Christmas shopping season in the Crescent City. Thanksgiving was a New England Protestant holiday, a substitute for Christmas in Puritan areas where Christmas had either been banned or ignored for many years. By the mid-nineteenth century some states outside of New England were celebrating Thanksgiving, but it had to be declared a holiday each year by the state's governor.

In 1863, Pres. Abraham Lincoln declared Thanksgiving a national holiday to be celebrated on the last Thursday in November. But in the post-Civil War South, Thanksgiving was at first disregarded by many people as a Yankee holiday. By the end of the nineteenth century Thanksgiving gained momentum as the beginning of the Christmas shopping season and was being embraced north and south. Pres. Franklin Roosevelt changed Thanksgiving to the fourth Thursday in November to extend the Christmas shopping season.

In New Orleans one kickoff to the holiday season is the annual Thanksgiving Turkey Day Race, presented by the New Orleans Track

Club. This footrace was originally sponsored by legendary sports coach and organizer Tad Gormley in 1908. Thanksgiving is also the day when the New Orleans Fair Grounds traditionally opened for a season that closes around Easter. In 2008 the venerable racetrack changed its opening to a few weeks before the traditional turkey day.

As Thanksgiving became more of a fixture for the start of the Christmas season in New Orleans, the Battle of New Orleans ceased to have any connection to the end of the holidays. In Confederate New Orleans an American victory no longer had the appeal it once had, particularly since the former enemy, Britain, had shown support for the South. The collective memory of the veterans of the Battle of New Orleans and even their children was fading, and even with the city's large anti-British Irish population, negative feeling toward Britain was fast disappearing. As King Cotton ruled the city's economy, much of the cotton wealth was financed by British banks and sent through Liverpool to the textile mills of Manchester. New Orleans' wealth was forged by British interests and new friendships were being made, ending decades of enmity.

Social Concerns of the Holiday Season

As the nineteenth century progressed, a spirit of caring took over many aspects of life in America and this was especially true at Christmas. A probable influence was the popularity of Charles Dickens' immortal tale *A Christmas Carol*, published in 1843. As Christmas became more of a children's holiday, the belief grew that every child should have a tree and a toy or two from Santa Claus.

There was also a growing expectation that the rich had a responsibility to help look out for the less fortunate. An editorial in the *Daily Picayune* shows how the spirit of Charles Dickens had come to permeate the holiday season in the Crescent City. "O rich man," the editorial asked, "did you think [of] . . . those others who looked out with wide eyes of wistful wonder upon the juvenile wealth of the more fortunate? . . . If one is richer . . . his motto must be noblesse oblige . . . the duty of relieving those inequalities. . . . Those, we trust, are wholesome Christmas reflections in keeping with the spirit of the day."

The Salvation Army was founded in London in 1865. It wasn't until 1891 that their first Christmas kettle was set up in America in downtown San Francisco. The idea soon spread to other cities, including New Orleans, and by the new century there were Salvation Army Christmas kettles in front of Canal Street stores.

New Orleans had a history of epidemics such as yellow fever, and losses from the Civil War had left many widows and orphans. Their predicament resulted in the establishment of group homes. Orphanages were recipients of much kindness at holiday time. In 1890 the girls at the Camp Street Female Orphan Asylum received useful gifts such as hair combs, new shoes, and stockings, along with more personal items. In the reception hall of the home was a Christmas tree

The Times-Democrat's Doll and Toy Fund provided a means for New Orleanians to donate money for the purchase of Christmas presents for the poor children of the Crescent City. Among the 1907 donors were a young future journalist/historian Charles L. "Pie" Dufour ($1), J. T. Gibbons ($10), "Peter Pan and Tinker Bell" ($2), and Don Juan Norvell, a bull terrier (80 cents "collected from his friends"). Even after the newspaper was merged to become the Times-Picayune, the Doll and Toy Fund has continued. (Louisiana Division/City Archives, New Orleans Public Library)

Thousands of poor white children line up in Lafayette Square to receive gifts from the Times-Picayune Doll and Toy Fund on December 23, 1922. In those days of racial segregation, gifts for black children were distributed at a separate event a day later. (The Historic New Orleans Collection)

where Santa Claus gave out presents. The wife of the president of the nearby Jewish Home added to the merriment by delivering cakes and sweetmeats.

In 1895 the ambulance corps of Charity Hospital acquired a Christmas tree for the children's ward. With great ceremony, decoration of the ward began at 3 P.M. on Christmas Eve. Around the tree were gifts donated by toy and clothing dealers from all over town. Even the poor youngsters from the neighborhood were invited to enjoy the party and receive a toy. If a child asked for a toy that wasn't under the tree, one of the ambulance drivers went out to try to satisfy the child's wish.

Santa Claus, wearing the appropriate attire, made his way to hospitals and orphanages laden with presents and sometimes Christmas trees. In 1900 the *Daily Picayune* described the arrival of the jolly elf at the children's Christmas party at Charity Hospital. "All of a sudden," said the article, "Santa Claus, a real life Santa Claus fresh from Greenland and frozen regions of the north pole, came bounding into the room. He carried an immense pack of toys on his back."

Adults in need were also worthy recipients, especially the elderly. In 1904 the aged ladies living at the home of the Little Sisters of the Poor received twenty-five turkeys along with baskets of fruits and other holiday edibles. The Jackson Brewing Company even came forward with coffee and beer. Gifts of all kinds were given in such abundance that there were leftovers.

In 1910 the Volunteers of America (VOA) gave its first free Christmas dinner for the poor in New Orleans. Maj. F. C. Fegley sent costumed Santas into the streets to solicit funds, and Fegley even spent some of his own money to make sure this first dinner was a success. The doors at the VOA hall, 121 Carondelet Street, opened on Christmas morning and the building was quickly filled by some of the city's poorest families. When food ran out, more was acquired to feed the more than two thousand people who attended.

The Doll and Toy Fund is a local effort to do good at Christmastime. The *New Orleans Times-Democrat* newspaper began the fund in 1896 and in the twenty-first century the Doll and Toy Fund is still sponsored by the *Times-Picayune,* which was created with the merging of the *Times-Democrat* and *Daily Picayune.* Originally held at the Washington Artillery Hall in the 700 block of St. Charles Street, the event enabled as many as ten thousand children to receive toys. The crowd of youngsters was so large that barriers had to be set up along the streets to keep everyone in order. A huge Christmas tree stood in the center of the hall and each year a prominent member of the community played Santa Claus. Each child also received a nickel for streetcar fare, and for those from the Westbank, a free ferry ride. Beginning in 1918 the gift distribution took place in a large tent in Lafayette Square until the event was moved to Pelican Stadium in the 1920s.

In the age of racial segregation the Doll and Toy Fund, along with other Christmas toy distributions, did not always include black youngsters. They usually received gifts through drives conducted by black New Orleans churches and fraternal organizations. The

WWL radio and later television personality Henry Dupre is shown with local children and Santa in a 1956 promotional photo for the Toys for Tots campaign. (Courtesy of Dominic Massa)

Times-Democrat began the Christmas Gift Fund for black children in 1913. In its early years gift distribution took place at the Knights of Pythias Hall on Saratoga Street, but it was moved to McDonough 35 High School on South Rampart at Girod Street in 1917. Almost seven thousand children attended the festivities. Along with the white Doll and Toy fund, it was relocated to Pelican Stadium.

In an editorial the *Times-Picayune* commented that through the fund Christmas cheer could be provided to children who live "within the shadow of poverty and otherwise would miss their share of childhood's Christmas heritage." The two toy distributions have been merged as one and are now held at the New Orleans Morial Convention Center. Toys for Tots, a national effort run by the United States Marine Corps Reserve, has also become part of the local holiday season.

New Year's Eve

Prior to World War I, New Year's Eve was just a continuation of the mayhem that began on Christmas Eve the week before. In 1903 the *Daily Picayune* said that the city was a "howling personification of pandemonium during the hours from dark to 1903," and the old year of 1902 expired with a "tremendous roar."

Just as on Christmas Eve, Canal Street was the center of activity. The great street blazed with light. Crowds of people rushed about and crowded each other while blowing horns, ringing bells of all sizes, shooting off Roman candles, and bombarding the air. Around 11:45 P.M. the sounds grew steadily louder, and then at midnight ships, steamboats, and anything that could make a noise added to the "deafening tumult," and just like on Christmas Eve, revelers were sometimes hurt by falling bullets.

By the end of the nineteenth century marching bands were appearing on New Year's Eve. All over town residents would open their homes to these marchers, providing refreshment and a rest stop.

Theaters staged special New Year's Eve presentations that ended just before midnight so their patrons could celebrate the stroke of twelve elsewhere. For many theatergoers the next stop would be the hotels that offered special banquets and dances to ring in the New Year. In 1912 the corridors of the Grunewald Hotel (later known as the Roosevelt, then Fairmont, and again Roosevelt) were jammed with partygoers, and all over the building "mirth reigned supreme." At midnight every light in the hotel was turned off. Especially popular was the hotel's nightclub, called the Cave, a fashionable night spot located in an actual basement (rare for New Orleans since its below sea level location made basements prone to flooding) designed to look like a cave, complete with plaster nymphs and gnomes. In the hotel's more sedate main dining room incandescent lights were flicked on proclaiming, "The Grunewald Wishes You A Happy New Year." Other hotels and restaurants such as the St. Charles, Cosmopolitan, Kolb's, Fabacher's, Antoine's, and Galatoire's were packed with celebrants.

New Year's Day

While the celebration of Christmas may have been limited to spending time with only immediate relations in a respectable nineteenth-century Creole family, New Year's was a time to welcome all friends and visitors. New Year's Day was a far more general and festive holiday than Christmas with its more solemn religious observance. It was a day of open house, as doors were open all over the Crescent City, and parlors were set with decorated cakes, bowls of eggnog, and sometimes even a showy and substantial lunch. Young gentlemen were expected to pay homage to young ladies of their acquaintance who spent the day at home receiving guests. Indeed, the mistress of the house was supposed to be at her most elegant and best advantage dispensing the hospitality of the home. In 1859 the *Picayune* hoped that the "pleasant custom of making visits will be observed . . . and that all the ladies will be at home and ready to receive."

Author Eliza Ripley recalled New Year's of the 1840s as the "visiting day for men, and receiving day for the ladies." The ladies "received in state," and gentlemen "donned their 'stovepipes' and proceeded to fill the society role for the year." Gentlemen, for whom it was an annual social duty for many years, went all over town either afoot or in carriages wearing their finest suits, kid gloves, polished leathers, and toppers. Ripley remembered the "endless procession of callers" that arrived all day long at the rows of fashionable mansions on Canal Street, before Canal Street became a shopping mecca. Callers darted in and out of doors and went to as many houses as they could visit in a day presenting good wishes for the New Year and leaving calling cards and small tokens of esteem for some young ladies. Slim, pointed cornucopias of bonbons and *dragées*, almond candies, were often the tokens presented by callers. It was not unheard of for young ladies to quietly buy their own little *drageés* to make it appear that they had been visited by more *beaux* than they really had.

Architect T. K. Wharton chronicled his enjoyment of the observance of the New Year's visitation and believed that one should see as many friends that day as possible. He thought the tradition should be cherished. In 1854 he noted that his wife received guests on January 2 because New Year's Day fell on a Sunday, making Monday "the Jubilee" instead.

In 1855, Wharton found people everywhere to be in the "highest spirits, and every house full of smiles and hilarity." In 1857 he noted that the streets were filled with men going quickly from one house to another, remarking that he made twenty-four house calls himself, ending up visiting friends at the St. Charles Hotel at 10:00 P.M. Two years later he noted that he only made twenty-one calls, but he seemed

Elaborate desserts were set out for guests who would come calling on New Year's Day during the middle to late 1800s. This elegant setting is the dining room of Gallier House Museum, former home of nineteenth-century architect James Gallier, Jr. (Photo by Syndey Byrd)

During the middle 1800s visiting friends and family on New Year's Day was a popular ritual. Eggnog has long been associated with the Christmas season and was especially popular in the South, as shown in this illustration from an 1870 Harper's Weekly. *In New Orleans both Creoles and Anglo-Americans regarded the often-spiked drink as genteel enough for all members of the family to enjoy. (The Historic New Orleans Collection)*

pleased with himself since he walked over three miles to make them in "mire . . . worse than a storm on the Atlantic."

In 1856 the *Daily Picayune* referred to New Year's Day as "pleasant and kindly" with its custom of family reunions and the rekindling of relationships that may have lapsed a bit during the past year. It was a day for the "abandonment of past enmities and the restoration of broken friendships." In the words of the *Daily Picayune* in 1870 "there was sunshine in the hearts of our people . . . around the family board. . . . All that was genial in the heart warmed into life and came sparkling through the eyes. . . . Those are New Year looks for you."

Along with a day of visiting, New Year's Day was also an important day of gift giving for Creoles. The *Daily Picayune* suggested that readers check the advertisements in the newspaper, remarking, "The proper thing to buy, and where they may be bought, are duly set forth in the ample columns of today's *Picayune*."

For Creole youngsters New Year's Day was especially exciting, since this was when the finer, larger, and more expensive gifts were given out when compared to the smaller trinkets placed in Christmas stockings on Christmas morning. On New Year's Day little girls were likely to receive beautifully dressed French dolls with china heads or porcelain tea sets, while the boys got lead soldiers, guns, rifles, or hobby horses. In the late nineteenth century there were the newest tin and cast-iron toys that were becoming increasingly more available in toy departments.

In some Creole families children presented parents with *complement de jour de l'an*, a brief verse in French to welcome the New Year. This was not unlike today's special handmade Christmas card, but a proper *complement de jour de l'an* was supposed to be written on decorated pink paper and presented in a pink envelope. This family ritual was followed by breakfast, which was similar to the Christmas morning breakfast of foods such as grillades (made with round steak, beef, veal, or pork) and grits and *pain perdu,* or lost bread (a type of French toast).

Breakfast was followed up with visits to the homes of godparents, grandparents, other older relatives, and then friends. Gifts were exchanged. In the early part of the nineteenth century New Year's Day generally ended quietly at home, but as the *réveillon* became more popular on Christmas Eve and Christmas night, it also became a part of New Year's night. Befitting the more jovial aspects of the New Year, these late-night affairs often included lavish food and drink and might last until dawn.

By the twentieth century most businesses were closed on New Year's Day and the bulk of the day was made up of visits to family and friends and the drinking of eggnog. The rushing about of young men making their visits and distributing calling cards was dying out.

During the nineteenth century, newspaper delivery boys conveyed to readers the message that they depended on tips through "carrier addresses" for the New Year. The addresses were sometimes elaborately illustrated like this one from the New Orleans Times-Democrat that welcomed in 1888. (The Historic New Orleans Collection)

In 1912 in her memoirs an elderly Eliza Ripley fondly recalled the old days of visits and greetings in the 1840s. She was saddened that ladies in the early 1900s simply put card holders on their front doors and callers would whisk by dropping off their cards while the ladies retired inside. New Year's Day of 1912, Ripley thought, was "dull" and "stupid" since "everybody who was anybody was out of town." Unlike New Year's of her youth, there was nobody in the streets since all the shops and businesses were closed—different from our own twenty-first century when many big stores and malls remain open having sales. Even the "pretty trifles" of candy cornucopias and *drageés*—which she had not seen in sixty years—she found to be relics of the past. The tradition faded rapidly, she believed, due to two reasons: it had not only become too much to do in one day, but it had spread to the "the outskirts of society."

Since 1947, thousands have gathered in Jackson Square on the Sunday before Christmas for a holiday sing-along presented by the Patio Planters, a French Quarter civic association. (Photo by Syndey Byrd)

CHAPTER FOUR

Christmas in the French Quarter

Red bows tied around shiny brass carriage lamps, holly wreaths hanging from ornately carved cypress doors, tiny white lights outlining a lemon yellow Creole cottage—talk about gilding the lily! But that's the way it is in New Orleans' French Quarter during the Christmas season.

The Quarter's narrow streets are paths to visual surprises, especially on the stretch of Rue Royale filled with antique stores, art galleries, and small shops. A timely portrait of the Madonna and Child in one window, holly-shaped earrings in another, a pleasing mix of gorgeous and gaudy.

Shopping, dining, or stopping to listen to street musicians is part of the scene year 'round but during the Christmas season, French Quarter Festivals, Inc., an organization that presents other events throughout the year with its primary thrust the French Quarter Festival in the spring, coordinates and stages myriad events under the banner "Christmas New Orleans Style." With support from the New Orleans Tourism and Marketing Corporation, efforts to draw visitors during what is typically a slow time of the year include free concerts at St. Louis Cathedral, cooking demonstrations, and attractive hotel rates. If you already live here, all this activity certainly enhances the holidays.

Historical Characters

If you run into a couple who look like they just stepped out of the 1800s walking down the street, they are part of the Louisiana Living History Project. A few weeks before Christmas, famous characters from New Orleans' past entertain visitors with vignettes from their own lives, songs, and an occasional dance. Legendary Voodoo priestess Marie Laveau may impart a few words to the wise; Jean Lafitte, the crusty pirate who helped Andrew Jackson win the Battle of New Orleans, will give you an earful. The characters' strolls include visits to the lobbies of local hotels and restaurants.

During the Christmas season, costumed characters from Louisiana history perform throughout the French Quarter. The group is known as the Louisiana Living History Project. (Photo courtesy of Gloria Powers)

House Museums

Through December many of the Quarter's historic house museums are decked out in Christmas finery. Hermann-Grima Historic House, 820 St. Louis Street, depicts life during the holidays in the 1830s through the 1860s with cooking demonstrations on a regular basis.

Gallier House, 1132 Royal Street, is also in holiday dress. Once the home of noted architect James Gallier, Jr., the house museum provides a glimpse into New Orleans in the 1850s.

During the Christmas season, the Beauregard-Keyes House, 1113 Chartres Street, literally gets "all dolled up." This 1826 structure, once the home of novelist Frances Parkinson Keyes, is decorated in Victorian style and touts an extensive doll and teapot collection. There's a holiday event called Tea Party for the Dolls that includes storytelling and a sing-along.

The Williams Residence is among the many buildings that comprise The Historic New Orleans Collection. An important museum and center for local history research, the home of its founders, Kemper and Leila Williams, has been maintained in the manner in which they lived during the 1940s and '50s. The staff puts up a tree in the home and decorates the residence and courtyard. Italianate in design, the elegant and understated home, built in 1889, is located at 718 Toulouse but access is through the Collection itself at 533 Royal Street. The Shop at the Collection features costume jewelry based on some of the treasures in their archives.

Also check out the Friends of the Cabildo Gift Shop, 523 St. Ann Street along Jackson Square. Both stores have locally themed items and a helpful local book selection.

St. Louis Cathedral: Concerts and Midnight Mass

During the Christmas season, under the Christmas New Orleans Style banner, there's a series of concerts held at St. Louis Cathedral at Jackson Square. One night, gospel, the next rhythm and blues, jazz, or classical. All free.

Right in front of the Cathedral, on a Sunday evening before

The historic Beauregard-Keyes House features a Tea Party for the Dolls during the Christmas holidays. (Photo by Syndey Byrd)

The Williams Residence, the home of late philanthropists Mr. and Mrs. Kemper Williams, is part of the complex that comprises The Historic New Orleans Collection. During the Christmas holidays, the home, which has been left exactly as the Williamses lived in it in the 1940s and '50s, is decorated for the season. (Photo by Jan Brantley)

Christmas, thousands gather for a giant sing-along sponsored by the Patio Planters, a French Quarter civic association. The group has staged the event since 1947, distributing candles and song sheets. The collective "glow" of the crowd with the Cathedral as a backdrop makes for a quintessentially New Orleans Christmas card setting. (This group also sponsors a Holiday Home and Patio Tour.)

Only a few days later, folks come together inside the Cathedral on Christmas Eve for Midnight Mass, continuing a ritual that goes back to 1718, New Orleans' first Christmas. To the left of the Cathedral's main altar is a life-size crèche, donated in the late 1990s by Nell and Harry Leveque, the original owners of the French Quarter-based Santa's Quarters store. It was made in Italy and is hand painted. There is an identical crèche at Jesuit Church (Church of the Immaculate Conception). Note the pre-Raphaelesque red-headed angel.

Midnight Mass has been a ritual of Christmas in New Orleans since the founding of the city in 1718. Here New Orleanians celebrate mass at St. Louis Cathedral. (Courtesy of the Clarion Herald*)*

One of New Orleans' most popular Christmas traditions is the annual caroling at Jackson Square. (Photo by Frank Methe)

Visiting crèches like this one at St. Louis Cathedral has long been a part of the holiday season. This crèche, made in Italy, was donated by the Leveque family. (Photo by Peggy Scott Laborde)

The Santa Rampage

On the Sunday before Christmas, there's a more recent "tradition" that can only be described with tongue firmly implanted in cheek. It's called the "Santa Rampage." A dozen or so gents dressed as St. Nick, accompanied by an entourage of Mrs. Clauses and people dressed as elves and reindeer, travel from bar to bar "elbowing" shoppers off the sidewalk and "snarling" at young children, hurling such comments as "Outta the way, kid," and "Got a cigarette for Santa?"

Attorney Keith Hurtt, Santa for a day, distributes switches and lumps of coal to the naughty. "To those who haven't been naughty," he says, "I offer condolences and wish them better luck next year."

"Our departure from various bars is usually signaled by a bell or by my friend Ian 'Claus' yelling, 'On Donner, on Dancer, andouille, ennui,'" adds Hurtt.

The rampage usually ends up with one of the "reindeers" who calls herself "Dancer" dancing on the bar at the Erin Rose, a French Quarter Irish bar.

On the Sunday before Christmas, a group of friends dressed as Santas descend in jest on various bars in the French Quarter in what they call the "Santa Rampage." Shown are "Santas" Ian McNulty and Keith Hurtt. (Courtesy of Ian McNulty)

A decorated balcony is a common sight in the French Quarter around the Christmas holidays. (Photo by Peggy Scott Laborde)

The French Quarter's Royal Sonesta Hotel lavishly decorates its lobby for the holidays. (Courtesy of the Royal Sonesta Hotel)

Holiday Inns

The halls are decked in the lobbies of many of the larger French Quarter hotels. Decorated trees and fancy foliage are staples at the Royal Orleans, 621 St. Louis Street, and the Royal Sonesta, 300 Bourbon Street. The latter holds Royal Teddy Bear Teas at this time of the year. During these special teas, Mrs. Claus tells holiday stories and of course Santa makes an appearance. A parade of characters led by a toy soldier trumpeter marches around the ballroom and each child receives a teddy bear and has the opportunity to take a photo with Santa.

On the two weekends before Christmas over at the Monteleone Hotel, 214 Royal Street, there's the Monte Lion Holiday Tea that includes lion-shaped sandwiches, music, games, and photographs with Santa.

The city's culinary traditions are in high gear during the Christmas season. Inspired by the after-Midnight Mass French Creole meal that

A Christmas tree and other decorations are displayed in the lobby of the Omni Royal Orleans. (Photo by Peggy Scott Laborde)

Mrs. Claus tells Christmas stories during the Royal Teddy Bear Teas held at the Royal Sonesta Hotel. (Courtesy of the Royal Sonesta Hotel)

Santa sits next to a French Quarter lamppost at Santa's Quarters on Decatur Street. (Photo by Peggy Scott Laborde)

was enjoyed by nineteenth-century New Orleanians, the term *réveillon now* applies to fixed-priced fancy meals at many Quarter restaurants and around town. Coordinated by the French Quarter Festivals, Inc. Christmas New Orleans Style, other food events include cooking demonstrations that take place in December at the Shops at Canal Place.

Shopping Christmas

Santa's Quarters at 1025 Decatur Street has been around since 1978. The store is a spot to find ornaments that have a regional touch. Ornaments shaped like crawfish, purple and gold treasures with Louisiana State University's logo, and the fleur de lis symbol that has come to symbolize the city of New Orleans are all hanging on the store's Christmas trees. Nativity scenes, traditional ornaments, garlands, wreaths, and lights are also available. This is a pretty comprehensive place.

For smaller, funky gifts, especially at the last minute, check out the

A magnolia wreath is a reminder that early New Orleanians used local greenery for their Christmas decorations. (Photo by Peggy Scott Laborde)

The French Market's Flea Market features many one-of-a-kind stocking stuffers. (Photo by Peggy Scott Laborde)

This French Quarter balcony on Dumaine Street has a message for all. (Photo by Sydney and Cathy Arroyo)

French Market's Flea Market. Good stockings stuffers include colorful molded plastic pins from local artist Oscar and actually decent silk ties. While the Quarter is filled with stores that provide many options for Christmas shopping, of particular note is the Dutch Alley Artist's Co-op. Located at 916 N. Peters behind the French Market in what is called Dutch Alley (after late New Orleans mayor Ernest "Dutch" Morial), the gallery is managed and operated by the artists themselves. Over twenty artists have their work on view.

Gilding the lily? More like gilding the holly and mistletoe.

CHAPTER FIVE

Decorated Homes

During the mid-1940s through the mid-1960s, as Christmas grew nearer, everyone in the family would get bundled up to take a ride to see some of New Orleans' most elaborately decorated homes. Some of those lights were in the Gentilly neighborhood, illuminating residences that belonged to the Gambino and Cigali families. In the Garden District there was the David home. The David family home at St. Charles and Washington Avenues was an enormous 1850s Greek Revival residence with stately fluted columns. A decorated tree stood on the second-floor balcony. Flanking it were streamers of colored lights. Next door was an enormous life-size Nativity; the Three Wise Men had already come a calling before Twelfth Night.

Across town in Mid-City was a must-see home that actually caused traffic jams. And it all goes back to a woman who got her decorating ideas from children's books. Mrs. Myra Collins Centanni, her husband

The David family home's Christmas decorations on St. Charles Avenue was a holiday highlight for many years. (Courtesy Brian David)

The Centanni Home on Canal Street

One of the must-sees when families would take rides around town to view Christmas displays during the mid-twentith century was the Centanni home. This art nouveau-inspired house belonged to the owners of Gold Seal Creamery, famous for its Creole cream cheese. Myra Collins Centanni and her husband, Salvador "Sal" Centanni, so lavishly decorated their Mid-City home that it became a showstopper. Salvador "Sammy" Centanni, Jr., the youngest of the couple's seven children, shares his memories of decorating the family home.

Q: What are some of your earliest memories of Christmas?

A: The first real year I remembered it, I had to be ten, twelve years old. I remember coming back from a trip with an aunt to Mobile and, gee, my house was all lit up. I couldn't

Mr. and Mrs. Salvador Centanni lavishly decorated their Mid-City home on Canal Street from 1946 to 1966. (Courtesy of Mr. and Mrs. Salvador Centanni, Jr.)

Not to be missed during the Christmas season was a visit to the life-size Nativity scene next to the David home on St. Charles Avenue. (Courtesy of Brian David)

Sal, and their seven children decorated their terraced art nouveau-style home at 4506 Canal Street, on the corner of South Murat Street, from 1946 until 1966. The family began putting up the elaborate display the day after Thanksgiving. Many a baby boomer recalls an almost life-size papier-mâché elephant whose trunk moved up and down. That concept came from a book about Santa going to a circus, according to son Sammy. Through the years visitors enjoyed Santa's workshop, complete with mechanized elves sawing and hammering; a life-size Nativity scene; and a Santa popping out of the Centanni home's chimney, as well as a Santa on the adjacent lawn in a sleigh led by papier-mâché reindeer.

The family's efforts inspired a little boy who often visited the home at Christmastime. In an interview in the 1990s, Al Copeland recalled how his own decision to elaborately decorate his home for the holidays developed: "It goes back to when I was a kid. I lived in the projects. We didn't have any money and we used to go look at Christmas lights every year. There was a particular home on Canal Street called the Centanni home . . . and [we] used to go there every year and I'd see it and say, 'You know, one day, if I have the money, I'm going to do this.' There was a period of time after Centanni's wife passed that he stopped decorating, ten years. I started doing it again, and picked up that tradition." Copeland, who founded the Popeyes Chicken and Biscuits restaurant chain, decorated his

The elaborate Christmas decorations on the porch of the Centanni home were a standout. Note the elephant. That year's theme was "Santa Goes to the Circus." (Courtesy of the family of Myra Centanni Mehrtens)

The decorated Centanni home on Canal Street in Mid-City attracted visitors from all over the city. (Courtesy of the family of Myra Centanni Mehrtens)

wait to get inside and see what it was all about.

Q: Who in your family initiated this idea of decorating?

A: This was my mother's idea. My mother would always put a wreath on the door and a few colored lights around the porch. One day she was outside just enjoying her garden and a gentleman stopped and he wanted to sell her a Christmas decoration for the yard. He described it to her and she said, "Sure, bring it over. I'll purchase it from you." This guy was a hobbyist. He came by in a truck and he unloaded this thing, and it was probably the size of a desk, a good-sized desk. And then he put the other part on it and it was a windmill. There was a little window and you could look in it and cutouts of people were in the windmill decorating for Christmas. And my mother bought that thing from him and that was the focal point of our lawn. And then she added the Christmas sled and the Nativity scene.

Q: Looking at photographs, it looks like there were sometimes themes in the home's decorations. Tell me about that.

A: She'd go to stores around Christmastime and find children's books, and she found one, one year that said Santa's circus is coming to town and it showed Santa coming in on an elephant. So my mother would call up a lady she also had making stuff for her, and they made big elephants—I mean, it was a life-size elephant—and put that on the lawn with Santa Claus sitting on it. A few years later, it was around the launch of the NASA Space Program, she

Santa Claus stands next to a rocket ship at the Centanni home. That year's theme was "Santa Goes to Outer Space." (Courtesy of the family of Myra Centanni Mehrtens)

found a book that said Santa's gone to outer space. She did a theme with a rocket ship with Santa Claus standing by it, and that is how she got her ideas, just from children's books. She tried to make it for children to enjoy. That was her thing.

Q: Tell me about Santa's workshop.

A: That came out from a book she saw about Santa's workshop. We had a carpenter that did work for us, and she asked him if he could build something of this nature that we could peep in and he did it, and she would go downtown and buy real toys and put them in the workshop. There were little elves hammering. That was all my mom; she had a sister, my Aunt Yvonne, who would work all year and think of things to do with these Christmas decorations.

Q: Tell me about the Nativity scene.

A: It was just a big square building. My aunt's husband built a part of a barn. They bought mannequins, old mannequins from D. H. Holmes. My aunt was a seamstress. She would take old

Among the many decorations featured in the side yard of the Centanni home was a replica of a church. (Courtesy of the family of Myra Centanni Mehrtens)

In the side yard of the Centanni home was Santa's workshop, which included elves "hammering" out toys for children. (Courtesy of the family of Myra Centanni Merhrtens)

Metairie home each year with a different theme for more than thirty years. In 2003, Copeland even paid tribute to the Centanni home in his own decorations. He died in 2008. The Copeland family donated his lights to Lafreniere Park.

Let There Be Lights

In New Orleans electric lights as Christmas decor became popular early on. The city's first general use of electric lighting was an experimental row of electric arc street lights set along the Mississippi River near Canal Street in 1882. It was an instant success, drawing sightseers to the riverfront. Within a few years arc lights illuminated Canal Street, St. Charles Avenue, and progressively more streets as the old-fashioned gas street lamps were phased out.

In 1879, Thomas Alva Edison introduced the incandescent light bulb with its carbonized bamboo filament. This was the first practical light bulb and revolutionized the expanding lighting industry. On Christmas night, 1884, the buildings of the World's Industrial and Cotton Centennial Exposition in Audubon Park burst into light as thousands of incandescent bulbs were simultaneously switched on in what, up to that time, was among the nation's largest uses of incandescent lighting. New Orleans began its love affair with bright electric lights.

Businesses were quick to see the advantages of the new lighting technology and in the early 1880s began electrifying workshops, showrooms, and show windows. Lighting not only expanded the ability to work at night, but made stores and their displays more attractive. In the mid-1880s, D. H. Holmes Dry Goods Store was among the first to replace gasoliers with electric lights throughout the store and in its show windows. More lavish was the half-block-long expanse of illuminated display windows of Maison Blanche department store in 1897.

Thomas Edison is credited with erecting the first large-scale outdoor display of lights in 1880 at his Menlo Park, New Jersey, laboratory. Even in the later 1880s such strings of lights were something seen in only the largest cities and then not always on a very big scale. With the success of the electric light displays at the World's Fair in 1884, many Canal Street businesses and clubs in New Orleans quickly followed the trend and draped their buildings with incandescent light bulbs during both the Christmas season and on Mardi Gras night. The sight of thousands of blazing 25-watt bulbs along Canal Street, then considered one of the most impressively illuminated streets in the nation, must have been an exciting sight.

Not until 1895 was the Christmas tree in the White House of Pres. Grover Cleveland lit by electricity. Tree lighting was enormously expensive, requiring hand wiring by a trained electrician. It was at first clearly a status symbol reserved for commercial establishments and the homes of the wealthy. In New Orleans, while Christmas lighting was in such commercial establishments as the St. Charles Hotel, bigger department and dry goods stores, and a limited number of wealthy

Central to the Centanni's Christmas decorations was the Nativity scene. It was donated to City Park and for many years served as part of its Celebration in the Oaks display. (Courtesy of the family of Myra Centanni Mehrtens)

Carnival costumes like duke's costumes with the capes—my dad was involved in Mardi Gras—and she made the Kings', the Wise Men's, costumes.

Q: When did you all start decorating your house?

A: We started it every year right after Thanksgiving. We would start digging lights out of our basement and opening the strings and plugging them in to make sure that they were all alright and changing light bulbs. Everybody had a job; we'd even bring some people from our creamery who would work at night. We would bring them in the daytime to help with the thing. And it was all done by hand and my dad supervised it, but when it got too big we had to get an electrician. We started blowing fuses and we had to get a special panel just to handle the Christmas lights.

Q: Now of course you're living in the middle of all this. What was your perspective from inside the house?

A: It was just as much fun inside as it was outside. My dad would walk to the front door and he would peep through the curtain, and he'd look and turn around and he would say, "Hey, Mom, we got a good crowd tonight," stuff like that. I will never forget there was a cotton candy vendor that ended up on the corner one night. My mother was upset at first. She said, "This is kinda commercial looking," and my dad said, "Oh, Maw, somebody's got to make a living, and it ends up our own children are his biggest customers."

Q: Describe the activity in front of your house during the Christmas season.

A: The cars would stop or even just drive on through or some would park and get out. We had a viewing area I guess sixty feet wide so people would just walk and gather and talk and look at it and point different things out to their children. They'd say, "Look at Santa on the roof," or "Look at the Nativity scene," and "Look in the church," but it was very exciting and we loved doing it just to see the smiles on the kids' faces.

Sunday evening the traffic was really great. It was bumper-to-bumper and sometimes police would stop by and try to direct traffic. But they would never rush people. They'd let people take their turn coming in slow. It all worked out and, to us, it never was a problem.

Q: Did your parents ever take your brothers and sisters to see decorated homes?

A: They had two big houses out that way that they always compared ours to. They belonged to the Gambino family and the Cigali family. They were on Gentilly Boulevard, right past, I guess, the Franklin Avenue area

For more than thirty years Popeyes Chicken and Biscuits founder Al Copeland lit up his Metairie neighborhood.

Eleven-year-old Al Copeland, who became the founder of Popeyes Chicken and Biscuits, stands next to Santa with his friend Frank J. van Mullem. Copeland, who elaborately decorated his Metairie home for over three decades, died in 2008.

homes, it was also in a few large churches. By the 1890s the Episcopal Christ Church, St. Paul's, the St. Louis Cathedral, and the Church of the Immaculate Conception dazzled Christmas worshippers and other visitors with strings of twinkling lights.

Miniature lights were developed in 1895, and in 1903 the General Electric Company introduced the first pre-assembled "festoons" of Christmas tree lights similar to what we know today. As early as 1906 electric companies, including those in New Orleans, were advertising the use of these lights for both their beauty and safety. The advertising did not say how dangerously hot the newfangled lights burned.

Most families in the Crescent City still would have had to use candles on their trees since few families had electricity. In 1910 there were only 13,504 electric meters in the city and most of them would have been used by businesses. Many people did not yet trust electric lighting, fearing that it was a fire hazard. They preferred, instead, to use tree candles, which would often have little glass covers or be enclosed by miniature metal lanterns to contain the flame, although the fire danger was still significant. Light bulbs had low wattage and were no brighter than gas jets, and while there was an array of electric appliances on the market, most people chose to do without them.

As early as 1906 the New Orleans Railway and Light Company advertised the convenience and safety of the Edison electric Christmas tree lights, even though most homes were not even hooked up to receive electricity until the 1920s. (The Historic New Orleans Collection)

By the 1920s this was changing. The introduction of tungsten light bulb filaments allowed great increases in wattage. New entertainment appliances such as electric phonographs and radios became an incentive for people to electrify their houses. The electric company, New Orleans Public Service, Inc., offered free hookup and a few months of free service, much as cable television companies did decades later, to encourage families to electrify. After World War I new homes were finally being built with full electric wiring. Eighty-nine thousand electric meters were in use in New Orleans by 1926.

In 1917 a novelty lighting company began the national sale of brightly colored electric tree lighting kits. The new lights were safer than earlier varieties and an instant success. The world as well as New Orleans was on the way to producing

there. And that was a big thing. Mom and Dad would always take us for a ride on a Sunday evening, check out everybody else's decorations, you know. Not that we wanted to outdo anybody. It was just, we had to go see it.

Q: When did you take down the decorations?

A: We would try to do it to coincide with the Feast of the Three Kings, the sixth of January. We'd start taking it down after the sixth.

Q: When did you all discontinue decorating your home?

A: Our mother died at a party for my father on New Year's Eve, 1966, first day of the year 1967. His birthday was New Year's. And that was the last year we really did it. It was her project so that was our last year.

Q: I'm sure you've heard by now that Al Copeland directly credits going to see the Centanni house as inspiration for lavishly decorating his own home.

A: Oh, I think it's great. Our father died in 1995. At the funeral home, they brought in a big Christmas wreath and they set it in the room and plugged it in. It had Christmas lights all over. I said, "Where'd this come from?" So I went and looked and the card said it was from Al Copeland. It said, "To the real King of Christmas," and we thought it was wonderful.

The Christmas decorations in front of this uptown New Orleans home have a whimsical touch. (Photo by Peggy Scott Laborde)

waves of colored light to illuminate the Christmas season. In the 1930s hand-painted novelty lights designed as fruits, flowers, and Christmas and cartoon figures appeared on the market. Introduced in the middle of the 1940s, bubble lights became immensely popular. By the end of World War II the use of electric tree lights had become virtually universal in the United States. Candles were relegated to special occasions and became as much a rarity as electric lights had been a half-century earlier.

About the same time people began decorating the exteriors of their houses with lights. As early as 1900 there were miniature outdoor lights for sale, but not until the late 1920s were outdoor lights being made with safety features that allowed the average family to string them around their home. By the 1930s houses in New Orleans were being decorated with outdoor Christmas lights that showed up in trees, bushes, along porches, and under eaves. The city's post-World

Many homes in the French Quarter are decorated in tiny white lights during the Christmas season. (Photo by Sidney and Cathy Arroyo)

War II neighborhoods with their abundance of baby boomer children became especially bright with Christmas lights that were not only safe but inexpensive.

Even the horror of Hurricane Katrina and its floods more than a half-century later did not completely knock out New Orleanians' love of Christmas lights; it only dimmed it for a while. Households went ahead and decorated anyway, even if that home may have been a temporary FEMA trailer.

Today many homes along St. Charles Avenue are lit with tiny white lights. Public lighting displays in the area include Metairie's Lafreniere Park and the Kenner Magical Christmas Village, next to City Hall, 1801 Williams Boulevard. Also in Kenner are lavish home displays from Maine to Texas Streets (just off David Drive and West Esplanade). The largest lighting display in New Orleans is the annual City Park Celebration in the Oaks (see Chapter 12).

A Nativity scene, Santa, and a snowman are among the charming decorations in the front yard of this Harahan home. (Photo by Frank Methe, III; courtesy of the Clarion Herald*)*

Displays of Greenery

Greenery such as holly and ivy has always been a part of decorating for winter festivals, and this was true of the Christmas celebration from its inception. In early times winter plants that grew wild were readily available for the picking and could be used in abundance to honor the season. During the nineteenth century, urban residents were increasingly far from the countryside and turned more and more to commercial florists and nurseries where specially grown decorative greenery was stocked throughout the holiday season. By the 1880s, Christmas trees were being shipped all over the country from tree farms, while poinsettias were being sold by plant dealers at the beginning of the twentieth century.

E. A. Farley's was a popular florist and nursery in Gentilly and was famous for its elaborate Christmas displays that attracted crowds of sightseers, as shown in this 1956 photograph by Franck-Bertacci Photography. (The Historic New Orleans Collection)

New Orleans florists have always done a thriving business selling Christmas plants, and to attract customers they often set up large displays. One notable establishment was E. A. Farley at 3333 Gentilly Boulevard. In the rear of the florist was a huge nursery that included blocks of greenhouses. It opened after World War II and not only helped beautify the gardens of Gentilly, but was also a popular destination for steady crowds of visitors who delighted in going to Farley's to see aisles of lavish foliage during both the Christmas and Easter seasons.

At Christmas, Elmer Farley, with his son Herman and daughters Orchid, Violet, and Lily, lined their shop with poinsettais and spun glass that resembled snow. They hung wreaths and garlands grown in the family's hothouses. Flocked and decorated Christmas trees were on display and of course were available for purchase. Some patrons may recall a Santa arriving at Farley's by helicopter.

After Elmer died in 1958, family members ran the business and continued the holiday tradition until the florist closed in 1980. The site was sold to Brother Martin High School, but many New Orleanians will remember that Christmas wonderland in Gentilly and the family that worked so hard to create it.

CHAPTER SIX
Let It Snow

Popular Christmas songs such as "White Christmas" don't exactly resonate in semitropical New Orleans, where locals can pretty much count on one hand the times they've seen snow. This is a city where everything comes to a halt at the sight of a snowflake.

FLOAT 15

WALKING IN WINTER WONDERLAND

Walking in a Winter Wonderland, written by Smith and Bernard and published in 1934 by Bregman, Vecce and Cohn.

*Sleigh bells ringing, are you listening
In the lane snow is glistening*

*Portraying fur trees
House and snow
In float form we show it here
A reality New Orleans does not know*

The Krewe of Carrollton's Carnival parade theme in 1948 was Songs, and one of the floats depicted "Walking in a Winter Wonderland," which was captioned "A reality New Orleans does not know." (The Historic New Orleans Collection)

113

Official Records of Snow

A New Orleans Christmas can range from bitterly cold to so warm that to wear a white linen suit might seem more appropriate than wearing wool. In reality the weather for most Crescent City Christmases falls somewhere in between. The National Weather Service in New Orleans has only kept official records of cold and snow since 1871. As for earlier weather reports, we have to rely on newspaper articles, memoirs, and diaries. Some early weather events include a great freeze in 1825, six inches of snow blanketing the city in 1852, and an 1864 freeze reported by the *New Orleans Times* to be so brutal that it even froze water inside well-enclosed rooms.

Between 1871 and 1935 there were only fifteen occasions when a trace of snow came down. Several of these occurred during the holiday season, although none on Christmas Day.

This postcard of Canal Street from the 1890s depicts a rare New Orleans snowfall. (Louisiana Division/City Archives, New Orleans Public Library)

Mayor Chep Morrison used this view of Jackson Square during the snowfall of February 1958 for his Christmas card later that year. (Louisiana Division/City Archives, New Orleans Public Library)

New Orleanian Maria-Kay Chetta is shown in front of her home in the Gentilly neighborhood during the New Year's Eve, 1963, snowfall. (Photo courtesy of Maria-Kay Chetta)

The 1963 New Year's Eve snowfall blankets a reindeer and other decorations at the Centanni home. (Courtesy of the family of Myra Centanni Mehrtens)

A White New Year's Eve

Snow blanketed New Orleans on Tuesday, December 31, 1963. A weatherman was sent from the Weather Bureau office to the lawn in front of the Union Passenger Terminal on Loyola Avenue where he raked away some flakes and measured the distance between the top of the grass to the high point of the snow. He measured 3.6 inches of the fluffy white crystals.

The fall of snow began about 3 A.M. on that Tuesday and continued unabated until the early evening, snowing for nearly eighteen hours. Not just a local event, it also snowed in Jackson and McComb, Mississippi, and Montgomery and Mobile, Alabama. This was the second time it had snowed in New Orleans that season; a week earlier there had been a flurry, but it was so slight it wasn't worth measuring.

Traffic was severely congested throughout New Orleans during the afternoon as businesses closed early. Most overpasses, underpasses, and bridges were shut down, although the Greater New Orleans Bridge over the Mississippi River remained open and jammed with traffic. It took hours instead of the usual minutes to drive home. There was a rash of traffic accidents and as New Year's Eve celebrating picked up, the numbers increased accordingly. Races at the Fair Grounds were canceled for the day when jockeys refused to take their horses on the slippery, snow-covered course.

Even though it created problems, the white stuff also provided amusement. Snowmen sprang up all over the city. There were many playful snowball fights while locals went out to look at the already picturesque city covered with a deep mantle of white. New Orleans resident Maria-Kay Chetta was a little girl then: "I put some snow in a little plastic container and put it in a freezer. I do recall having that for years—just didn't want it to go away—and also we rode around looking at everybody's snowmen. Someone had dyed a snowman with food coloring and that was really something to see."

With freezing weather there were the inevitable problems: frozen pipes, ruined gardens, and ruined New Year's Eve plans. The snow continued falling into the evening and then it stopped, to be replaced by a brisk, dry wind. This enabled partygoers to venture forth. Canal Street was thronged as usual.

This snow-covered angel was part of the Centanni home's decorations during the New Year's Eve, 1963, snowfall that left almost four inches of the icy stuff on the ground. (Courtesy of the family of Myra Centanni Mehrtens)

A rare snowy day in Audubon Park on New Year's Eve, 1963. (Photo by Frank Methe, III; courtesy of the Clarion Herald*)*

Audubon Park under snow on New Year's Eve, 1963. (Photo by Frank Methe, III; courtesy of the Clarion Herald)

The French Quarter received its share of the white stuff on New Year's Eve, 1963. Pictured is the courtyard of the Court of Two Sisters restaurant. (Photo by Catherine Arnold; courtesy of the Clarion Herald)

As the day wore on and with almost four inches of snow, the Fair Grounds finally had to shut down on New Year's Eve, 1963. (Photo by P. H. Guarisco; courtesy Louisiana Division/City Archives, New Orleans Public Library)

Snow became a problem when the New Year's Eve, 1963, snowfall left Tulane Stadium's football field covered with the white stuff the day before the Sugar Bowl was to be played. Its removal was documented by photographer Leon Trice. (Gift of the Sugar Bowl; courtesy of The Historic New Orleans Collection)

An Alabama cheerleader jumps in mid-air with a snowy field as backdrop during the Sugar Bowl on New Year's Day, 1964, when Alabama defeated Mississippi following one of New Orleans' heaviest snowfalls. (Photo by Leon Trice, gift of the Sugar Bowl; courtesy The Historic New Orleans Collection)

Bourbon Street, which had been closed to traffic, was jam-packed with revelers who gave restaurants, bistros, and bars standing-room-only business.

Across town at Tulane Stadium more than four inches of white blanketed the gridiron. With this much snow there was concern that the next day's Sugar Bowl game might have to be canceled. To ensure that the match between Alabama and Ole Miss (University of Mississippi) was played as scheduled, twenty-five maintenance men worked through the night clearing the stadium. Boy Scouts pitched in to sweep and shovel the aisles. Orleans Parish prisoners were mustered, while trucks from New Orleans Public Service, Inc., spread hot sand. Snow was successfully shoveled off the tarpaulin covering the field and piled on the sidelines. Alabama defeated Ole Miss 12 to 7.

As a freeze, the New Year's snow was not very impressive. The temperature remained around 32 degrees all day long as the snow accumulated and dropped only into the mid- to upper 20s during the night after it stopped snowing. In spite of the not-so-freezing temperatures, this weather event remains New Orleans' "great snow of the twentieth century."

It was nearly ten years before measurable snow again fell on the city. This time it was almost an inch on February 9, 1973, marking the second snowfall of that year. A few flakes had fallen on January 11.

Traffic gridlocked hopelessly in places, as everyone tried to get home on this Friday afternoon when offices, stores, and schools all closed early. Making matters worse, visibility was greatly hindered by flurries. There were over four hundred traffic accidents reported across the city.

Bridges and interchanges were closed as surfaces became icy. Many workers were simply trapped downtown, and as a result French Quarter restaurants did a roaring business. On the other hand, movie theaters did not do so well. A hundred reservations were canceled at the Trans-Lux Cinerama on Tulane Avenue, while at the Lakeside Theatre No. 1 in Metairie no one showed up. The telephone company appealed to people via television and radio to limit their telephoning. Phone lines were clogged and emergency calls needed to get through.

On Friday, December 22, 1989, an Arctic cold mass poured south across the United States, freezing pipes, highways, and gardens. The *Times-Picayune* proclaimed, "Worst Freeze in six years drops in for the holidays." Shelters opened for the homeless, and even special heated areas were set up to provide extra warmth for the animals at the Audubon Zoo.

According to the *Times-Picayune*, "People stopped wrapping Christmas gifts and started wrapping pipes." Folks rushed to hardware stores to snap up insulation and plastic sheeting to protect the exposed plumbing underneath their homes. Not everybody was so lucky since many families had already left town for Christmas, leaving their houses unprotected against the cold. When the frozen pipes thawed, they began to crack; water spewed out as if from a fountain from under many New Orleans homes.

This was the heaviest snow in sixteen years. Although it was only

New Orleans City Hall employees enjoyed a rare New Orleans snow (almost an inch) in February 1973. A few flakes had also fallen in January of that year. (Louisiana Division/City Archives, New Orleans Public Library)

about an inch deep, it made driving hazardous. Ramps in some high-rise parking garages were iced over, causing cars to practically slide down to street level. Parts of Interstate 10 were closed, as was the Westbank Expressway. Mayor Sidney Barthelemy urged businesses to close early, which had the unfortunate effect of clogging downtown. It took hours for most commuters to get home. Many without rides were forced to walk when buses stopped rolling and taxis became difficult to find.

Maria-Kay Chetta vividly remembers being in the middle of the traffic mess: "When that hard freeze came and the streets were freezing over, I remember they said, 'You can go home.' I was working at the police department on Broad Street and we all went out and I'll never forget: I was at Jefferson Davis Parkway and Canal Street and my car started to slide and I thought, 'Well, if I turn it off, I won't slide,' not realizing it's the ice. I'm thinking if I turn the motor off, the car's just going to stay in one place. But it was still sliding. I passed all kinds of people, off to the side, smashed into cars."

"It really shut the city down, but we had a ball. It wasn't quite enough to make a snowman but we tried," recalls Grammy-winning vocalist Irma Thomas. "We made some little bitty snow people."

Apart from the hazardous aspect of this act of nature, there was also fleeting, or more apt, sleeting beauty. Uptowner and New Orleans historian Sally Kittredge Reeves explains, "I will never forget how beautiful St. Charles Avenue looked covered with snow in 1989. The old houses were emerging from this blanket. And the oak trees were standing blanketed in snow. You couldn't see the asphalt in the street and so it was very pretty."

In an interview for WYES-TV, author Anne Rice, then living in the Garden District, recalls, "I was writing *The Witching Hour* and I ran to the window and I looked out at. The entire lawn was capped with snow. My son had gone out skating in his tennis shoes and had written in giant letters, 'I love you Mom and Dad' in the snow, which I thought was great. I ran right to the typewriter and I added snow in *The Witching Hour*. And so *The Witching Hour* contains scenes, key scenes at the end, where Michael is having a terrific battle with the villain in the snow and the ice and actually falls in the ice-cold, half-frozen swimming pool. And no one has ever questioned this, but it is a fact. It actually snowed. I wouldn't have dared to put a fictional snowfall in New Orleans."

By Saturday morning, December 23, the temperature fell to 12 degrees, a bit below the 12.5 degrees set in January 1962 and the lowest since 1899, when the city's record low fell below 7 degrees. In spite of this, Christmas shoppers managed to find their ways to shopping malls in the cold yet sunny weather. Crowds were impressive and sales were brisk, and one woman interviewed at Lakeside Shopping Center said, "I didn't expect it not to be this way. It's Christmas."

On the morning of Christmas Eve it was predicted that the temperature might fall as low as 5 degrees to break the all-time 1899 record. This did not materialize, as the low only fell to 15 degrees, which merely broke the 1983 record.

By Christmas Day the temperature pushed toward the 50s. Snow in sheltered areas stayed around a little while to provide a white Christmas, but not for long. The day after Christmas, normal, mild winter temperatures returned to the Crescent City. Maria-Kay Chetta further recalls, "I remember on Christmas Day there was no water. I remember having to eat our Christmas dinner off paper plates."

Citywide many thawed pipes were breaking and spewing water. One plumbing firm had a waiting list of more than one hundred names and was serving only regular customers. In Jefferson Parish, where several water mains broke, thousands of homes were without any water pressure.

At Last, a White Christmas!

On Christmas Day, 2004, a large dome of Arctic air was in place over southeastern Louisiana when a band of moisture moved in to create perfect conditions for snow across New Orleans.

The day was marked by a leaden gray sky when, in the middle of Christmas afternoon, a wet and frigid sprinkle of snow came down. It was less than an inch, but it offered a rare spectacle. Some families took advantage of it and built snowmen, although the gents were on the tiny side.

Writer and photographer Ian McNulty snapped this photo on Christmas Day, 2004. He recalls that day in his book, A Season of Night: New Orleans Life After Katrina: *"I spent the day at a friend's house in the Treme, the beautiful, historic but drug-scarred neighborhood just north of the French Quarter. We did the snowball bit ourselves. We ran up and down a block that on a normal day we would traverse only with caution and an eye out for thugs. At the corner of the block, a barroom door opened and out walked Kermit Ruffins, a trumpet player and an endlessly gregarious New Orleans character who channels the spirit of Louis Armstrong in his jazz shows and everyday demeanor. He stepped outside wearing a Santa Claus hat and carrying a Budweiser longneck in one hand and his shining trumpet in the other. He stood on the corner for a minute with his fiancée. As the snow sailed down, blurring over the evidence of neglect on the ancient Creole cottages around us, Kermit put his lips to his trumpet and blew a few bars of 'Silent Night' before breaking into his well-known, benevolent laugh and taking a pull from his beer. It was one of those rare and wonderful moments that, even as it was happening, I knew would have a special place in my memory forever."*

As pretty as the snow cover was for people who ventured outdoors to enjoy the dreamlike occurrence, others were faced with less pleasant challenges. Flights from Armstrong International Airport were canceled, Interstate 10 was closed from Kenner to Baton Rouge, and there were numerous traffic accidents.

As the afternoon wore on, driving conditions worsened, as most roads in and out of the city were shut down. Icy conditions forced city buses to be halted in mid-afternoon. By the next day, only a few shady pockets still had snow. In most places it had either melted or turned into layers of slippery ice waiting to be melted by the sun.

The snowfall of December 11, 2009, added a wintery touch to the crèche in front of Notre Dame Seminary in New Orleans' Carrollton neighborhood. (Photo by Mitch Semar, courtesy of the Clarion Herald)

Little did anyone know that such a weather rarity would foreshadow another weather rarity eight months later: the ferocity of Hurricane Katrina.

The winter of 2008-9 proved to be one of America's snowiest in recent years, and New Orleans received a small and unusual share of it. Even television's Weather Channel included the New Orleans snow among the five most notable winter events of the season. A fast-moving cold front collided with damp air along the Gulf Coast, producing a "snowstorm" that fell from Texas to Alabama, blanketing southeast Louisiana along the way. On December 11, 2008, a few lonely flakes of snow began to fall on New Orleans at about the peak of the morning rush hour, but soon big fat wet flakes began to cover the city. As drivers eased along slick roads, some downtown pedestrians got the rare sight of wind-driven snow swirling around the green Christmas wreaths decorating Canal Street's tall light standards. Snow blanketed automobiles, rooftops, yards, and parks. A few miniature snowmen popped up. Although power was knocked out in many areas, especially on the Northshore, most businesses and schools opened for business as usual. By mid-morning the snow soon turned to sleet. An inch of snow fell, but it quickly melted, since the temperatures were a little above freezing. At two weeks before Christmas, it put everyone in the Christmas spirit and left New Orleanians with one more snowy memory to treasure.

This 1870s bonfire at Laura Plantation in Vacherie, Louisiana, is the earliest known photograph of a bonfire along the Mississippi River upriver from New Orleans. (Courtesy Laura Plantation Company)

CHAPTER SEVEN

Bonfires and Beyond
New Orleans

Nearly forty-five miles from downtown New Orleans, there's a winter ritual that has survived for over a century and a half with roots that go back much further. It's the setting of Christmas Eve bonfires on levees along the Mississippi River.

Today, the majority of the bonfire activity takes place on the east bank of the river in St. James Parish, with some in St. John the Baptist, St. Charles, and Ascension Parishes. Willow, cane reed, and other tree branches are used to construct what amounts to wooden sculptures, most resembling a teepee but others much more elaborate. More than one hundred structures are ignited at the stroke of seven. Popular belief holds that this tradition originated as a means of lighting the way for Papa Noël or lighting a path to church for Midnight Mass, but recent research shows the ritual's beginnings are a bit more complex.

"The bonfire tradition in Louisiana is probably the oldest, longest-lasting tradition of celebrating Christmas in North America," says Norman Marmillion, owner of Laura Plantation Company in Vacherie. "It started with our ancestors, my ancestors, who came to this area in the 1720s around Germany and France along the Rhine River. They brought with them this two-thousand-year-old tradition that the Celts had of burning bonfires at the winter solstice and the summer solstice. The Catholic Church took over the Celtic winter solstice and called it 'Christmas'—when light is coming back into the world, darkness will not take over. A bonfire is that celebration and you get this very deep feeling that something magical is happening."

The communities of Gramercy and Lutcher are where much of the activity takes place, with Gramercy hosting a Festival of the Bonfires in early December. The event includes a gumbo tasting, local bands, amusement rides, and a small bonfire. Funds raised are used to pay for liability insurance for the Christmas Eve bonfires.

Ancient Roots

In Europe the winter solstice is the darkest and coldest time of the year. Until the late nineteenth century, a blazing fire was the only way to cut the dark and cold, so fire, such as the tradition of the yule log, has been an important part of most winter festivities. Fire was also

One Christmas Eve

Rhythm and blues guitarist/ bandleader Deacon John Moore has performed in the New Orleans area since the 1960s. Here he recalls performing upriver in the town of Donaldsonville early in his career.

A club owner would call us to play every Christmas Eve in Donaldsonville, Louisiana. It was called the Town and Country Club. I remember the guy's name was Tony Falsetto. Great club manager. Just a great guy. Now before we would start—we'd start playing around ten—he'd tell us, "You have to take a break around 11:30. And come back around 12:30, see, 'cause all the people leave and go to Midnight Mass and then they come back and party." I couldn't believe this. I said, "What?" Just as sure as he said, we'd start playing all the Christmas songs, "Please Come Home for Christmas," all that Christmas music. And then all of a sudden, everybody would clear out. The whole joint was empty. They all came back after Midnight Mass and started partying again.

believed to expel evil spirits, just as noise, fireworks, and gunfire were used to drive away evil spirits on the holy eve of Christmas.

Ancient France, Germany, and the British Isles were all under the influence of the Celts, and while the Celts were not united as a nation, their culture was universal across Europe and a dominant force from about seven hundred years before the birth of Christ until it was overtaken by Christianity. As part of the Celtic tradition, huge fires were built to honor the sun and harvests and are still built for midsummer festivals in such places as Alsace in France and across the border in neighboring regions of Germany.

The word "bonfire" is thought to be a corrupted version of the term "bone fire," derived from old English, literally meaning a fire made of animal bones. This ritual of burning bones came about during the ancient Celtic festival of Samhain, which occurred annually at the end of October, the beginning of the Celtic New Year. Samhain was also a commemoration of the harvest and the shortening days of autumn. The burning bones were supposed to ward off evil spirits. Our modern Halloween most likely evolved from this important Celtic festival.

From the Celts' winter solstice festival we continue to use holly and mistletoe, something sacred to the Druids (the Celtic priestly class), along with the yule log, as part of the celebration of Christmas.

With the passage of time coupled with the growth of Christianity and the celebration of the birth of Christ, it may have been a simple evolutionary step to move bonfires from autumn and Halloween (bonfires still mark the celebration of Halloween in parts of the United States) to winter and Christmas Eve to not only cut the cold, but also provide light and drive away demons on this joyous night.

Louisiana's Christmas Bonfires

The earliest settlers who came to Louisiana from France and Germany in the 1720s were from areas where bonfires were lit at Christmas. In sections of France, there was the burning of fireballs, torches, and bonfires along with burning the yule log, which in French is *bûche de noël*, although today this term usually refers to a cake shaped like the log, rather than the log itself.

With the settlers in the upriver parishes, according to Marmillion, "We know that the preceding weeks of Advent had a strictly religious focus, certainly no rushing around buying gifts. The bonfires would, in a sense, kick off the Creoles' [holiday] season, getting everyone in the family involved, leaving the austerity of Advent behind, with lots of food preparation, drinking, music, and dancing."

A merchant who collected shipping-box wood all year long built bonfires at the New Camellia Plantation on Christmas Eve in 1844. An 1871 photograph taken at Laura Plantation shows people around a bonfire. According to Marmillion, the photo was taken "on the levee next to the river and people are dressed up. It's probably the oldest photograph [of the bonfires in the area] we know of. We have written records of the bonfires, of people coming in for parties, a lot of dancing, drinking. The River Road bonfire tradition originally included two annual celebrations, each six months apart: December 24 and June 23 [St. John's Eve], both set aside for family reunions and religious reasons."

Marcia Gaudet, a folklorist and assistant professor of English at the University of Louisiana at Lafayette, has extensively researched the bonfires and indicates that Marist priests in the 1880s introduced bonfires to Convent, Louisiana. The late Emily Chenet Guidry, a noted expert on the history of St. James Parish and author of *Bonfires on the Levee,* interviewed elderly residents of the upriver parishes and concluded that the earliest Christmas Eve bonfires in these parishes date to the late nineteenth century. There are others who recount memories of bonfires on the levee in the early years of the twentieth century, but these bonfires seem to have been very few in number and built by individuals rather than part of some sort of a concerted community effort. One elderly respondent recalled that more affluent plantation owners had built the fires.

Waiting until dark can be a challenge for those eagerly waiting to ignite the bonfires on Christmas Eve, but the rule mandates that they light their pyres at 7 P.M. sharp. (Photo by Syndey Byrd)

This steamboat design is one of many shapes that shows the creativity of bonfire builders. (Courtesy Durel Millet)

Christmas bonfires along the Mississippi River levee near New Orleans may date back to the nineteenth century, but they did not become a major event until after World War II. Today they have become an important tourist attraction. (Photo by Syndey Byrd)

Papa Noël

The widely held belief that the bonfires were meant to help lead Papa Noël on his Christmas Eve rounds sounds charming but has little credence. Papa Noël, like Père Noël, as a children's gift giver may have been derived from the Christ child but is more likely a French interpretation of the American creation of Santa Claus. These figures did not appear until the last decades of the nineteenth century—and then did not grow in mythical stature until the early twentieth century. By this time Santa Claus had come to rule even across Louisiana. Also, within the French tradition it was more common, even into the twentieth century, for gifts to be given on New Year's Eve, with Christmas gifts and Papa Noël playing a secondary role. Prior to the twentieth century many rural families were too poor or isolated to even include gifts as part of their Christmas.

The Growth of a Tourist Attraction

Emily Chenet Guidry's research points out that in the years between World War I and World War II more residents started building small fires upriver on Christmas Eve. During this time the families on the Welham Plantation began building bonfires of sugarcane reeds, to which they later added scraps of wood. The early fires took place in the pasture but were later moved to the levee.

During World War II the burning of bonfires went into hiatus, but after the war ended they returned with growing popularity. They became more standardized, with willow branches being the most popular wood used since it grows in abundance along the riverbank. Cane reed was another standard addition because it is hollow, similar to bamboo, and when ignited makes a popping sound.

Boys formed bonfire clubs, cutting and gathering the necessary wood. A stout center pole was selected and sunk into the ground on the top of the levee. Additional center support poles were angled to form the desired shape of a tall pyramid. Logs were then placed within the support poles. Today deemed environmentally hazardous, discarded rubber tires were once used as kindling. Fireworks are still added to the tall pyres to add more smoke and noise. Might this be a derivation of the noise used to drive away demons in the ancient manner?

Prior to World War II, there were few people living in the vicinity to enjoy the fires. With the increased use of automobiles, new highways, and river bridges this all changed, drawing crowds to witness the annual blazes that become more and more popular with each Christmas. The growing audience comes mostly from New Orleans, Baton Rouge, Houma/Thibodaux, and even Lafayette and the Mississippi Gulf Coast. There are now riverboat cruises and bus tours.

Building bonfires is a coming together of family and friends. Construction often begins as early as Thanksgiving, although with a

Christmas at Oaks Plantation

New Orleans historian Sally Kittredge Reeves recounts her paternal grandfather's Christmas memories as a college student at the turn of the twentieth century on a sugar plantation along Bayou Lafourche. Dr. Willoughby Eaton Kittredge was born at Oaks Plantation near Napoleonville.

My grandfather grew up on a sugar plantation on Bayou Lafourche out in the country, which is really less romantic than it sounds because it was quite lonely, especially for children, young people who long to have and join in festivities. They developed a custom which drew back, I think, into the nineteenth century of inviting their college friends, their friends from the city, to the plantation for Christmas house parties, which lasted up to two weeks. They played charades all day and got dressed up in costumes and enjoyed each other's company out on the big old galleries in front of the house.

At night they went to the sugar house, which was humming with activity during grinding season of course, and the big vats of sugar looked as dark as the River Styx. It was boiling and bubbling and dirty; it was something you definitely wouldn't want to fall into, and the catwalks around the edges above all these works were available for the young adventurous people to climb all over. They actually had wonderful parties, music and food in the sugar house in the midst of all the humming activity. So it was lots of fun for them to invite their friends from town.

And low and behold, one Christmas my great-aunt invited her college friend to the country . . . a young woman, a young Creole, French Creole from New Orleans, and she met my grandfather and the rest was history. So they met at one of these Christmas house parties. My grandfather graduated from Tulane medical school and ultimately moved back home where he practiced medicine and raised sugarcane.

lot of hard work and a lot of help it can be done in three or four days. For some families it has become a ritual that has been passed down from father to son. St. James Parish resident Gerard Roper, now in his forties, has been building bonfires for a long time. "I've been doing this since I was a little kid, and my kids have been doing it since they were little kids. So it's a family tradition that's been going on since I've been living here, and I've been living here all my life."

Roper remembers the days before the height restrictions, enacted in 1991. "When I was a kid, we had one probably fifty feet tall, if not taller. We used to build them way bigger than what we build them now. It was sort of dangerous, but back then we started after Halloween. So we had a lot of time to do it, and then you had wood available because you didn't have all these subdivisions like you have now. So you had woods to go in to get the material. We used to haul the wood with bicycles. We had knives and bow saws to cut the wood. Now it's a lot easier with pickup trucks and chainsaws." While it has traditionally been a man's job, now women are getting involved in the building process.

In St. James Parish alone there are about 140 permits for bonfires issued each year, and the permits are tightly regulated. Precursors of today's bonfire builders would probably have been appalled at the thought of having to apply for a permit to build a fire.

Among the more creative bonfire designs in recent years was one shaped like the Louisiana State Capitol. Note a gentleman dressed as Huey Long in front. (Photo by Syndey Byrd)

*Every year Laura Plantation hosts a bonfire party to kick off the Christmas season.
(Courtesy of Laura Plantation Company)*

Bonfire builders would often let their imaginations run wild; they would model their structures after all sorts of monuments, ships, and famous buildings. Some pyres were reputed to have reached sixty feet. As a precaution, officials were forced to mandate that all bonfires be built in the safer teepee shape and not exceed a more modest eighteen feet. Of the more than one hundred bonfires built each year, only three structures are allowed to be built in a non-traditional style. In the more recent past, designs have included a miniature replica of the Louisiana State Capitol, a plantation house, ships, and an airplane. All these activities are under careful observation by local firefighters.

On Christmas Eve, 2005, just months after Hurricane Katrina inundated most of New Orleans, a bonfire structure shaped like a helicopter was built in honor of the National Guard's rescue efforts. That same year many of the structures were built out of some of the enormous amounts of debris left in the wake of the floods.

Sparks fly, there are popping sounds from the cane reed, and an occasional firecracker—sights and sounds that are a mysterious yet welcoming continuum from ancient days to future nights on the levees. "It's just a time of year you look forward to," says Roper. "It's hard to explain. It's just tradition, it's something we do. We enjoy doing it. I couldn't imagine Christmas without it."

Christmas on the Plantations

Upriver from New Orleans are several plantations that recall the history of an economy that was supported by slave labor. Prior to the Civil War, along with the *Daily Picayune's* wishes for a merry Christmas

Christmas celebrations on Southern plantations prior to the Civil War could be jolly affairs with eating, drinking, and dancing enjoyed by both master and slave. The holiday provided slaves with a few days' respite from their usual toils, as seen in Frank Leslie's Illustrated Newspaper *in 1857. (The Historic New Orleans Collection)*

and its many advertisements for Christmas gifts were more sobering ads for auctions of "Valuable Slaves, House Servants, &c." At that time New Orleans had a relatively small black population—about 14 percent of 168,000 in 1860—and only about half of this percentage was free. Many free people of color were Catholics and had French Creole roots. For most of them Christmas was scarcely different from that of their white Creole counterparts. In many households and plantations the slaves were included in its celebration.

The *Daily Picayune* on December 21, 1858, reported that servants in Carrollton, then a separate community with farms and dairies, were given a Christmas ride to town on the Carrollton railroad, complete with music and singing. On one plantation in the area, revelry, according to the newspaper, began Christmas morning and lasted throughout the night. There was music and dancing, the distribution of new clothing, as well as sports in which even the master and mistress might take part. Eliza Ripley recalled in 1859 at Whitehall Plantation that "Christmas

Day, the field negroes were summoned to the back porch of the big house where Marse Jim, after a few preliminary remarks, distributed the presents—a head handkerchief, a pocketknife, a pipe, a dress for the baby, shoes for the growing boy (his first pair, maybe)." Ripley said that often the slaves were asked ahead of time what they wanted and an order was filled in the city. Ripley remembered that the passing of a jug of whiskey followed the distribution of gifts. At Whitehall the slaves were given a week-long holiday and a trip to town, where they could do a bit of buying on their own.

For families living along the River Road, Christmas was a time of coming together and visiting with relatives they hadn't seen in a while. It was also a solemn celebration for many, as it was for their city cousins.

Today several plantations have been restored and stand as testament to the hard work and craftsmanship of the enslaved laborers. Some are decorated and have special activities during the holidays.

The magnificent 1846 Greek Revival Madewood Plantation House, located in Napoleonville, is home to a Christmas Heritage Banquet on the second Saturday in December. Caroling by candlelight is a highlight of the evening, which includes music performances.

Oak Alley, in Vacherie, is another antebellum Greek Revival

The festooned entrance to Houmas House hints at the elaborate decorations inside. (Photo by Kerri McCaffety; courtesy of Houmas House)

Even the staircase is beautifully decorated at Christmastime at Houmas House. (Photo by Kerri McCaffety; courtesy of Houmas House)

The stockings have been hung with care at the restored Houmas House in Darrow, Louisiana. (Photo by Kerri McCaffety; courtesy of Houmas House)

A Christmas tree sits in a parlor at Houmas House. (Photo by Kerri McCaffety; courtesy of Houmas House)

Owner Kevin Kelly has restored the 1840 Houmas House to its former glory and lavishly decorates the plantation at Christmas. (Photo by Kerri McCaffety; courtesy of Houmas House)

The table decorations at Laura Plantation were usually limited to what was grown on the plantation. (Courtesy of Laura Plantation Company)

plantation and is framed by a quarter mile of almost three-century-old oak trees. There's a fancy Christmas bonfire party on the grounds in early December.

Laura Plantation, a rare Creole-style structure that has been lovingly restored after a catastrophic fire, stages a bonfire and evening of caroling. According to owner Norman Marmillion, Laura is decorated in its original context. "For our annual Christmas party, because of the religious and family aspects; the decor is rather subdued by today's standards," states Marmillion. "We use only greenery from the plantation: magnolia leaves; cedar; pine cones; all kinds of berries in season, wild and cultivated; all kinds of nuts available; and any fruit and citrus still available on site." These floral items are used for garlands, mantel, and table decor. Of major importance is the traditional Christmas tree, which reflects the ethnic heritage of the early settlers of the area. Marmillion continues: "We know that the tradition on River Road of placing a small evergreen atop a table and

Young ladies from the Napoleonville area traditionally assist in the festivities at the Madewood Christmas banquet. (Courtesy of Millie Ball Marshall)

decorating it is the same custom followed today in the Rhineland. So our Laura tree is a small tabletop one, decorated in handmade lace stars holding images of Laura's family."

Houmas House in Darrow, Louisiana, is elaborately decorated for the holidays. This 1840 Greek Revival structure was restored by Kevin Kelly in 2003. A highlight is Latil's Landing Restaurant.

Destrehan Plantation in Destrehan, Louisiana, now stages a Christmas ball. Built in 1787, it is considered the oldest documented plantation in the lower Mississippi Valley.

Christmas is a hectic time of the year to say the least, but consider traveling up the River Road for yet another aspect of the area's holiday history.

This table at Laura Plantation illustrates the way Creole families quietly celebrated Christmas in the 1800s. (Photo courtesy of Laura Plantation Company)

CHAPTER 8

Food, Glorious Food

Food and its preparation are very much a part of life in New Orleans, and at Christmas this becomes even more apparent. From a winter festival whose roots include the harvest and the slaughter of meat before the onset of the cold, one of the holiday's most enduring traditions has become the overwhelming consumption of food and drink. Like Christmas itself, the dishes of New Orleans during its nearly three hundred years of existence have evolved. There are not only traditional dishes such as turkey in the United States and plum pudding from Britain that provide a national sense of community, but also family recipes that are prepared only at this time of the year and as a result are comforting in tasting "like Christmas." Just as everywhere else, Christmas is a time when expense becomes less of a concern.

That holiday tradition of culinary bounty has been extended to include sharing and concern for the needy. Today large charitable Christmas feasts such as those prepared in New Orleans at the Ozanam Inn and Bridge House are as much a part of the feel-good season as enjoying a bountiful feast at home or an elegant brunch in a restaurant or hotel.

Réveillon

The *réveillon* has recently been reintroduced into Christmas dining in New Orleans. The term is a derivation of the French word for "awake" and is generally a late-night meal following an event such as the opera, theater, party, or in the case of Christmas, Midnight Mass. In contemporary New Orleans the term most often is associated with a holiday meal special at a restaurant. In the mid-1980s, French Quarter Festivals, Inc., the organization that coordinates holiday activities under the Christmas New Orleans Style banner, conceived the idea of encouraging local restaurants to offer a festive fixed-price meal during the season.

Christmas Eve *réveillons* have been celebrated for centuries in France and such former colonies as Quebec and New Orleans. Historically they were small snacks or meals meant to break the fasting observed prior to Midnight Mass. During the nineteenth century the *réveillon* evolved into something grander and more formal. The meal took place

Brennan's Restaurant is one of many New Orleans dining establishments that features réveillon *dinners during the Christmas season. Now considered a fixed-price holiday meal, the term originally referred to a nineteenth-century New Orleans Creole late-night breakfast, usually eaten after Midnight Mass. (Courtesy of Brennan's Restaurant)*

in the home and was strictly a family affair. In the Creole culture, an invitation was highly prized, especially one to the home of a non-family member. The family component of the late-night *réveillon* was pointed out by the *Daily Picayune* in its Christmas issue of 1897 in an article titled "The Christmas Reveillons."

> To-night in almost every home in New Orleans old people and young will sit up to keep the merry Christmas eve. There is something essentially beautiful in these home gatherings, this clustering of hearts in loving sympathy around the yule log. Down in the French quarter there will be many merry gatherings and when the night is far spent a few moments will be snatched for slumber, and then will follow the midnight mass, when the sweet story of Bethlehem that never grows old will be told to waiting hearts. The inevitable tinhorn will be in evidence all night, and the noise of pistols and firecrackers. But for all that we love the dear old festival, that makes the heart glow with such tender thoughtfulness.

The meal that accompanied the Christmas *réveillon* was a fairly light one by the standards of a day when gargantuan feasts were common and would perhaps be better described as an early breakfast. Depending upon the size and wealth of the family, it could include several varieties of egg creations; of a heavier nature there were meat dishes such as grillades (a square of meat cut from a round steak, veal, or pork) with grits. Also on the table would be daube glacé, a jellied beef dish. There were several kinds of bread, including the famed *pain perdu*, a form of French toast.

As much for decoration as for consumption, molded desserts in elaborate designs, a European tradition, were very popular, and there were also cakes, some swimming in wine and topped with mounds of whipped cream. While most of the dishes were made at home, bakers in the French Market would sell special cakes for the Christmas holiday.

The French *bûche de noel*, a pastry shaped like a yule log, would also be a holiday staple. Rounding out the meal were fruits and assorted fruit dishes, wine, the inevitable Christmas eggnog, and coffee.

Creole New Year's Réveillon

For the Creoles of the Crescent City, the great holiday celebration was held on New Year's Day. Some families had a New Year's Eve *réveillon* that was more light hearted and festive than that held on the more solemn Christmas Eve. New Year's Day was a day of visiting and exchanging of gifts, and just as gifts then were more expensive than on Christmas, food was richer, more elegant, and dearer than that eaten at yuletide.

Bowls of eggnog were set out for visitors. There would be fruitcake

During the middle 1800s men would pay New Year's Day visits to relatives and friends. Eligible young ladies gauged their popularity by the number of cornucopias filled with sugar-coated almonds (dragées) *that they would receive from visiting young gentlemen. The setting is the historic Hermann-Grima Historic House. (Photo by Syndey Byrd)*

and dainty sweets such as sugarcoated almonds known as *dragées,* bonbons, small cakes, and pralines. Once the day of visiting ended in the early evening, the great Creole holiday meal began around 6 P.M. This meal was usually an elegant sit-down affair of five or six courses that, unlike the Christmas Eve *réveillon,* might include non-family members. It was a rich meal that usually revolved around such local favorites as turtle soup, gumbos, shrimp, and crabmeat. There might even be the all-American turkey—but stuffed with truffles, which were far less expensive than today. With the end of dinner came *brulé,* a flaming drink of brandy, kirsch, maraschino, cinnamon, allspice, and sugar, or *café brûlot,* coffee fortified with brandy, spices, and orange and lemon peel. Both drinks were set aflame, carrying out the Christmas season's disposition for fire, only this time in a bowl or cup.

Holiday Drinks

For many people drinking has long been a part of the Christmas celebration. During the late nineteenth century hard alcohol was frowned upon as a Christmas drink, and in some households liqueurs and cordials were thought more appropriate for mixed, multi-generational company. In New Orleans, hard drinks were considered more an American holiday tradition, while Creoles were predisposed to wines. Across the United States during the nineteenth century, holiday drinking and rowdiness was frowned upon by the middle classes, resulting in Christmas's becoming less of an occasion for intoxication.

In the United States, especially in New Orleans and the South, eggnog was a popular beverage synonymous with the holiday season.

Originally a non-alcoholic French concoction, it was quickly adapted by Anglo-Americans to their own tastes by mixing its eggs and milk with alcohol, adding usually rum and nutmeg. For a more respectable form of Christmas celebration the alcohol could be eliminated or left at a minimum, which made it palatable for gentlemen who wanted a drink but genteel enough for children and ladies who did not care to imbibe. This adaptable drink fit well with the Creole Christmas. A few sips of eggnog would be acceptable prior to Midnight Mass, when fasting might be observed, and then could also be consumed after mass at the family *réveillon.*

Throughout the entire holiday season, including the New Year, eggnog could be found on virtually every sideboard. In 1866 the employees of the *Daily Picayune* wished the proprietor of the St. James Hotel barroom "a hundred Merry Christmases" for sending "so bountiful an eggnog and such a good wine to grace it with all."

In 1901 the Christmas issue of the *Daily Picayune* gave its readers this recipe for "Old-Fashioned Creole Eggnog":

> Ten fine, fresh Creole eggs, one quart of milk, one pound of white granulated sugar, one gill [¼ pint] of fine French cognac, one grated nutmeg.
> Beat the yolks to a cream, add the sugar and beat to a cream. Blend all thoroughly, beating till very, very light. Now pour over the boiling milk, stirring well. When thoroughly blended add the whites of the eggs, beaten to a stiff froth, and the liquor, and serve hot. This eggnog is also served cold by the Creoles at New Year's receptions. At the famous Christmas and New Year reveillons it is served hot. The liquor may or may not be added, according to taste.

Not everybody had such mild holiday tastes, and for those individuals who wished more potent drinks in the late 1890s, when the age of the cocktail was coming upon us, the *Daily Picayune* listed a few fairly elegant, but probably potent Christmas drinks. These included the Mistletoe Punch, made of vermouth and whiskey with orange peel; the Yuletide Cream, of whiskey, lemon rind, sugar, and seltzer; the Christmas Joy, containing yellow chartreuse, absinthe, and Benedictine all shaken with egg yolk. Christmas Delight was made up of rum, brandy, and milk topped with a sprig of holly.

The Festive American Bird, Turkey, in Creole New Orleans

Turkey was a part of the New Orleans holiday dining experience from the city's first Christmas, in 1718. *Dinde* is French for a turkey hen, while the gobbler is called *dindon.* Discovering the bird during its North American exploits, the Spanish had introduced turkey to Europe in the sixteenth century, and the big festive bird soon found its way across the continent. There were European settlers who even believed turkeys to be native to Europe and got a surprise when they found them in such abundance in the New World. In the New Orleans area turkeys, some of them weighing as much as thirty pounds, roosted in trees.

In the late nineteenth century the markets of New Orleans, including the French Market, were filled with prime turkeys in great abundance on Christmas Eve and Christmas Day. Architect T. K. Wharton wrote of picking up his Christmas turkey on Christmas Day. There were also vendors who walked about town with small flocks of the birds, selling them for Christmas dinner. The animals made a considerable amount of noise and were purchased live, which meant that the bird was killed and dressed at the purchaser's home.

For the more traditional Creole families, turkey was not part of the Christmas *réveillon*, since this was a light meal, but it was certainly on view on New Year's Day, when turkey might be served elegantly trimmed at the evening feast. *The Picayune's Creole Cook Book*, first published in 1901 (and thereafter for decades), said, "The boned turkey is the triumph of the New Orleans cuisine. . . . It is the standing dish on New Year's Day, when Creole ladies receive their gentlemen friends." If this was indeed the case, young gentlemen making their numerous calls on New Year's Day must have become rather tired of the bird by the end of the day.

Dining Out at Christmas

By the mid-nineteenth century, in what was becoming a less Creole and more American New Orleans, there were fewer *réveillons* and more places to eat out on Christmas Eve as well as on Christmas Day since many hotel dining rooms and restaurants remained open. They offered Christmas meals that tended toward classical French and Anglo-American cuisine with little representation of local fare other than such seasonal items as shrimp, crabmeat, and various fruit.

An example of a holiday season menu was the one prepared for the Twelfth Night of 1854 at the St. Charles Hotel. Their dining room was considered one of the grandest restaurants in the country. Its offerings, written in French, were limited but quite elegant, including *galantine de dindon* and *dindon* stuffed with truffles. There were also mutton, duck, and trout. Such items as buttered asparagus and lyonnaise potatoes were offered between courses. There was fruit and cheese for dessert.

In 1872 the hotel's Christmas Day menu was much more extensive and included a wide array of meats, including beef, veal, and pork. Also part of the selection was corned beef and cabbage, along with the ever-present turkey.

By the end of the nineteenth century there were newspaper listings for the many local hotels and restaurants that provided special Christmas and New Year's menus. In the 1890s the then new Hotel Grunewald (later the Roosevelt) offered filet mignon, filet of the turbot fish, as well as the ubiquitous roast turkey with chestnuts and cranberry sauce. Various vegetables, salads, and desserts were available, including a Christmas staple even in New Orleans at the time—English plum pudding. At most hotels Christmas dinner was served between 5 P.M. and 8:30 P.M. The bill? Less than a dollar.

In 1909 the St. Charles Hotel had a menu similar to that of the Grunewald, with mostly American offerings, including young roast pig, roast mallard duck, roast ribs of prime beef, as well as roast turkey stuffed with chestnuts and served with cranberry sauce. Desserts included mince, lemon meringue, and pumpkin pies as well as plum pudding with hard and brandy sauces.

While restaurant and hotel Christmas dinners today sometimes include complimentary champagne, in 1909 the St. Charles offered its patrons crème de menthe punch to whet the whistle.

Christmas Day Home Cooking

By the end of the nineteenth century the holiday meal in most New Orleans homes would have been more in line with the Anglo-American tradition of a large Christmas Day dinner. While there were local touches, by now turkey had became a universally accepted part of the feast.

Each year the Christmas Eve issues of such newspapers as the *Daily Picayune* provided a Christmas menu on the Women's page. For Christmas breakfast the *Picayune* suggested orange slices, something in season in Louisiana but a luxury in colder climates, as well as the local favorite *café noir.*

For the main meal there were almost always some local delicacies. Especially popular as a beginning course were shrimp dishes and oysters on the half shell followed by roast turkey with cranberry sauce. Gumbos or jambalaya, which would eventually be found on more present day Christmas restaurant menus, were not regularly included in the newspaper suggestions, although in 1895 chicken gumbo was listed as a course between the first course of oysters on the half shell and the third course of baked red snapper. Roast turkey followed the snapper. In 1898 local dishes such as boiled shrimp, chicken sauté a la Creole, and stuffed sweet peppers were noted.

In 1901 the *Daily Picayune* printed its Christmas menu in French, but in the same issue it included recipes for English plum pudding with hard sauce along with a mincemeat pie, the ingredients of which even included beef, mutton, and suet (beef or mutton fat), rarities in many of today's more fruity American mince pies. On the 1901 menu there was also fruitcake, already a staple of the Christmas season.

The 1901, *The Picayune's Creole Cook Book* suggested a Christmas dinner that it described as an "old-fashioned Creole holiday menu, in vogue for generations among Creole families of moderate means." Here were listed such local favorites as gumbo filé, *court-bouillon* (a broth used to poach fish, seafood, or vegetables, locally it could also refer to a tomato-based fish stew), and *beignets d'oranges* along with more typical American and Southern fare like roast turkey—here with oyster stuffing—and cranberry sauce, sliced and buttered baked yams, mashed potatoes, stuffed tomatoes, lettuce salad with French dressing, and old-fashioned chicken pie.

The ingredients on the kitchen table in the 1860s Gallier House remind us that holiday meals began with a trip to the local market. (Courtesy of Hermann-Grima/Gallier Historic Houses)

For dessert New Orleanians generally feasted upon mince or apple pie; pineapple sherbet; sponge, jelly and pound cakes; apples; oranges; bananas; an assortment of nuts and raisins; cheese; crackers; and raspberry marmalade along with Creole bonbons and *café noir*. There was also plum pudding that may be considered British and not generally part of a New Orleans Christmas, though it would have been part of Christmas dinner for the city's British residents such as T. K. Wharton. Author Lafcadio Hearn included eight recipes for plum pudding, of which two were for Christmas, in his *Creole Cook Book,* published in 1885.

The sometimes-gargantuan menus of the late nineteenth and early twentieth centuries became a bit less extravagant as the twentieth century progressed. The Christmas menu found in Virginia M. Cooper's *The Creole Kitchen Cook Book,* published in 1941, included such local dishes as oysters on the half shell and gumbo filé along with roast turkey with Creole dressing, giblet gravy, and cranberry sauce; salad with mayonnaise; potato buns; crackers; celery; olives; rice; crackers; salted nuts; plum pudding; hard sauce; fruit cake; and of course, *café noir*.

Decorating the Table for Christmas

By the late nineteenth century sources such as cookbooks and newspapers offered suggestions to New Orleans housewives about how to decorate their dining rooms for Christmas dinner. In 1899 the *Picayune* called roses or holly the only "appropriate decorations for the Christmas table," but the newspaper found holly to be the preferable choice saying, "The beautiful red berries in the entourage of green leaves are very effective." Holly, it said, should deck the mantel and be looped through the curtains and a holly wreath should be hung above the fireplace. The *Picayune* even suggested holly be put in all the vases as well as a "great clustering bouquet in a low cut-glass bowl in the center of the table. The bright red berries against the dark green speak of the Christmas glow and cheer that fill the heart." The paper suggested that little gift packages for dinner guests might be hidden in the foliage of the centerpiece and long ribbons be attached to each gift extending to each table setting.

In 1941 local cookbook writer Virginia Cooper suggested red poinsettias, ferns, and red candlesticks as decoration. In a mere forty years poinsettias had become an important part of the American Christmas showcase since by this time the plant, native to Mexico, was being grown locally in hothouses and was readily available at nurseries as part of the ever-changing world of Christmas.

Rebirth of Les Réveillons

For restaurants Christmas Eve and Christmas Day business waned during the early twentieth century, as those days became more of

Nineteenth-century New Orleans housewives decorated their homes with greenery in preparation for their guests during the Christmas season. An example can be found at the restored Houmas House plantation on the outskirts of New Orleans. (Photo by Kerri McCaffety; courtesy of Houmas House)

an at-home-with-family tradition. This practice began to change in the 1970s as families began to look for Christmas dining experiences outside the home. Special brunches in hotel dining rooms with bountiful quantities of food and freely pouring champagne satisfied the New Orleanian seeking a holiday treat. By the end of the twentieth century these feasts had become popular family events in both hotels and restaurants at Christmas and other holidays. For those who still ate at home, many families let supermarkets and takeout establishments cook the dinner that might include Louisiana's contribution to the holiday feast, fried turkey.

Before the recent revival of the *réveillon*, most people knew of it only as a quaint old-fashioned Creole custom. However, while rare, some residents held on to the tradition. Growing up in the 1930s and '40s on the Northshore of Lake Pontchartrain in tiny Madisonville,

New Orleans restaurant owner Leah Chase recalls in a 2006 WYES-TV interview: "In the country what we had, we always had gumbo. We always had gumbo at festive meals. Coming home after mass, Midnight Mass, that's when we had what we called the *réveillon* and our *réveillon* would be to come home to stewed chicken and baked macaroni and some wine and sit up all night. We didn't go to bed on Christmas. Adults didn't go to bed on Christmas. So we had *réveillons* all night long."

In the 1980s this old French ritual officially returned to the Crescent City, but like so much else related to Christmas, it came back with a new twist. Through French Quarter Festivals, Inc.'s Christmas New Orleans Style promotional efforts, this once late-night private family affair has gone public and can now be experienced by everyone in the dozens of restaurants that offer nightly *réveillon* meals with four or five courses at a fixed price.

In 2000, David Armstrong wrote of New Orleans in the *San Francisco Chronicle:* "The holiday season is a fine time to visit this rollicking city; the smothering heat of summer is gone and worldly New Orleans takes on a family-friendly ambiance and innocence (well almost)." He describes how the modern *réveillon* "proceeds throughout December at an almost stately pace. It is warmly expansive, encompassing special *réveillon* restaurant feasts." The concept has become particularly popular with locals, creating a new tradition revolving around festive and abundant dining during the cool weeks of the holiday season.

Holiday Recipes

One adventurous young New Orleans cook tried to inject a bit of Victorian England into his family Christmas celebrations. New Orleans artist and musician George Schmidt recalls this childhood memory:

> I had just finished reading Charles Dickens, you know, *A Christmas Carol.* And I saw a movie version with Alistair Sim, playing at the Civic. So I said, "Well, I'm going to make a wassail bowl." So I went back into the kitchen and all that afternoon I was making this wassail bowl. And the book said you make it with ale and also some other things like brandy and I asked somebody and they said, 'Ale is like beer.' So I went out and I got a big six pack of Dixie Beer. So I used Dixie Beer in it. I was cooking it on the stove and it turned into this huge, gelatinous mass. It smelled of hot beer—that's what it smelled like—and I brought it into the party and nobody touched it, not a single soul touched this glue . . . it was this brownish glue!

Schmidt may have had little success with his culinary attempts, but here are seven recipes from some of New Orleans' finest chefs and cooks. Now let's really get cookin'.

Chef Jeremy Langlois' Bisque of Curried Pumpkin, Crawfish, and Corn. (Courtesy of Houmas House Plantation)

Bisque of Curried Pumpkin, Crawfish, and Corn

Chef Jeremy Langlois
Latil's Landing Restaurant, Houmas House Plantation

Chef Jeremy Langlois began his culinary career the day after his sixteenth birthday in May of 1995, when he joined Chef John Folse's White Oak Plantation team. Within seven months, he was promoted to prep cook. Langlois' mentor, Chef Folse, saw the enthusiasm and the potential in the young protégé and gave him a full scholarship to the John Folse Culinary Institute at Nicholls State University.

Chef Langlois was promoted to executive chef at the award-winning Lafitte's Landing Restaurant at Bittersweet Plantation at age twenty-two. Latil's, where Langlois works as executive chef, was recently named by *Esquire Magazine* as one of the top twenty best restaurants in America. There he masterfully creates wonderful dishes in a style that he calls "Nouvelle Louisiana."

Jeremy Langlois is the executive chef at Latil's Landing Restaurant at Houmas House Plantation. (Courtesy of Houmas House Plantation)

1 cup olive oil
2 cups chopped onions
1 cup chopped bell peppers
1 cup chopped celery
½ cup chopped garlic
1 cup flour
1 cup Steen's cane syrup
¼ tbsp. curry powder
2 qt. crawfish stock
2 cups fresh corn kernels
1 lb. peeled Louisiana crawfish tails
1 14-oz. can unsweetened pumpkin
1 cup heavy whipping cream
Salt and pepper to taste

In a large pot heat olive oil over medium-high heat; add onions, bell peppers, celery, and garlic. Cook until translucent, about 10 minutes. Stir in flour and cook for 2 minutes. Stir in cane syrup, curry powder, crawfish stock, corn kernels, and crawfish tails. Whisk in pumpkin and bring soup to a boil. Reduce heat and simmer for 30 minutes. Add heavy whipping cream and season soup with salt and pepper to taste.

Yields 12 servings, 6 oz. each.

Oysters Grand-Mére

Chef John Besh
Restaurant August, Besh Steak, Domenica, Lüke, and La Provence

Chef John Besh grew up in southern Louisiana learning the essentials of Louisiana's rich culinary traditions. He won the James Beard Award for Best Chef of the Southeast in 2006. His appreciation for local ingredients and local cuisine has only increased since Hurricane Katrina, as he considers these essential to the survival of the people and cultural heritage of New Orleans. Oysters Grand-Mére—from his maternal grandmother—and Spinach Madeleine, which follows, are family recipes.

1 cup chopped onion
¼ cup diced celery
2 oz. bacon fat
¼ lb. unsalted butter
¼ cup diced bell pepper
2 tbsp. minced garlic
1 tbsp. chopped parsley
3 tbsp. Creole seasoning mix
1 cup cooked crawfish tails, seasoned and minced
2 tsp. hot sauce
¼ cup green onions
3 qt. minced French bread
2 cups fried oysters, minced
1 cup raw oysters, chopped
1 qt. oyster liquor
4 eggs

Sauté mirepoix (the combination of onions and celery) in bacon fat and butter. Remove from heat and transfer contents to a mixing bowl. Add remaining ingredients and fold together. Pour into an oven-safe dish and bake at 350 degrees until golden brown.
Yields 4 qt.

Spinach Madeleine

Chef John Besh
Restaurant August, Besh Steak, Domenica, Lüke, and
La Provence

4 tbsp. butter
2 tbsp. minced shallots
1 tsp. minced garlic
2 tbsp. flour
2 lb. fresh spinach
½ cup heavy whipping cream
½ tsp. black pepper
¾ tsp. celery salt
½ tsp. cayenne pepper
1 tbsp. Worcestershire sauce
6 oz. Creole cream cheese
Salt and pepper to taste

Melt the butter in a 2-qt. pot over medium heat. Add shallots and garlic. Sweat the garlic for 5 minutes before adding the flour. Add spinach and cook for 3-5 minutes, stirring constantly until the spinach is wilted. Stir in cream, black pepper, celery salt, cayenne pepper, and Worcestershire sauce and simmer for 5 minutes. Add the cheese, then season with salt and pepper to taste. Mix well and transfer to a casserole dish. Reserve until ready to serve. Before serving heat the casserole in a 375-degree oven for 30 minutes.

Yields 12 servings.

John Besh is the proprietor of many New Orleans-area restaurants, including Restaurant August. (Courtesy of John Besh)

Chef Gus Martin's Paillard of Turkey with Cranberry and Caramelized Shallot Sauce. (Courtesy of Muriel's Jackson Square)

Paillard of Turkey with Cranberry and Caramelized Shallot Sauce

Chef Gus Martin
Muriel's Jackson Square

Muriel's Jackson Square chef Gus Martin has more than twenty-five years of culinary experience. Born in New Orleans, he began his career at the age of fourteen in the kitchen of Commander's Palace under the direction of Chef Paul Prudhomme. At Commander's he ultimately became executive sous-chef and moved on to the Palace Café as executive chef. Martin has also held executive chef positions at Dickie Brennan's Steakhouse and Ralph Brennan's Ralph's on the Park.

Gus Martin is the executive chef at Muriel's Jackson Square. (Courtesy of Muriel's Jackson Square)

Sauce
4 oz. shallots, minced
1½ tbsp. butter, divided
4 oz. cranberries
2 tbsp. molasses
3 cups chicken stock
1 tbsp. chopped fresh thyme
1 tsp. kosher salt

Caramelize shallots in 1 tbsp. butter, then add cranberries and molasses. Cook 5-10 minutes over low heat. Add chicken stock and reduce by more than half, cooking for 5-7 minutes. Whisk in remaining ½ tbsp. butter, fresh thyme, and salt.
    Yields 4 servings

6 oz. turkey breast
⅛ tsp. kosher salt
⅛ tsp. cracked black pepper
1 tbsp. flour
2 tbsp. cooking oil
¼ cup cranberry sauce

Season turkey breast with kosher salt and cracked black pepper, then dredge in flour. Heat oil in a medium sauté pan. Sauté turkey breast until golden brown, 5-7 minutes. Spoon sauce over turkey. Serve with mashed potatoes and haricots verts (French green beans).
    Yields 1 serving.

Crepes Fitzgerald

Chef Lazone Randolph
Brennan's Restaurant

Executive Chef Lazone Randolph has worked at Brennan's Restaurant for more than forty years. When asked for a recipe, he recommended the restaurant's Crepes Fitzgerald: "It's very festive and it's an exciting dish to complete a holiday meal."

Crepes
Melted butter for brushing
3 large eggs
1 cup milk
½ cup all-purpose flour

Lazone Randolph is the executive chef at Brennan's Restaurant. (Courtesy of Brennan's Restaurant)

Preheat a 5-inch crepe pan or skillet and brush it lightly with melted butter. In a medium bowl, beat the eggs with the milk. Add the flour and whisk until smooth. Strain the batter to remove any lumps. Pour about 2 tbsp. batter into the pan, tilting the pan to spread the batter evenly. Cook the crepe over medium heat until golden brown, about 30 seconds, then turn the crepe and brown the other side. Repeat the procedure with the remaining batter. Crepes can be sealed in plastic wrap and frozen for several weeks.
Yields about 16 crepes.

1 lb. cream cheese, room temperature
5 tbsp. sour cream
10 tbsp. sugar
1 tbsp. vanilla
16 crepes
1 tbsp. butter
5 cups fresh strawberries, stemmed and sliced
Juice of ½ lemon
2 tbsp. maraschino liqueur

In a mixing bowl, combine the cream cheese, sour cream, 2 tbsp. sugar, and vanilla. Beat until smooth. Spread 3 tbsp. of the cream cheese filling on one end of each crepe. Roll the crepes and refrigerate while preparing strawberry topping.
Place the butter and remaining 8 tbsp. of sugar in a large saucepan. Cook for several minutes over medium heat, stirring, until the sugar dissolves. Mix in the strawberries and lemon juice. Bring the mixture to a boil over high heat, then reduce heat to medium and cook for 10-12 minutes until the liquid thickens. Cooking time will depend on the ripeness of the strawberries. Add the maraschino liqueur and flame the mixture.
To serve, place 2 crepes on each plate and spoon about ¾ cup of warm strawberry topping over the crepes.
Yields 8 servings.

Next to its famous Bananas Foster, Brennan's Crepes Fitzgerald is one of the restaurant's most popular desserts. (Photo by Cheryl Gerber; courtesy of Brennan's Restaurant)

Bûche de Noël

Chef Tariq Hanna
Sucré

Pastry chef Tariq Hanna is co-owner of Sucré, a pastry shop inspired by the patisseries found in Paris. We asked him for his recipe of that most traditional of New Orleans Christmas dishes, the *bûche de Noël,* or yule log. Of course this dish has its roots in New Orleans' mother country, France.

Toasted Almond Cream
2½ cups + 2 tbsp. milk
7 oz. ground toasted almonds
1 tbsp. cocoa powder
½ cup + 1 tbsp. sugar
1 tbsp. vanilla extract
6-7 (½ cup) egg yolks
¼ cup cornstarch
1 cup (2 sticks) butter

Bring milk, almonds, cocoa powder, sugar, and vanilla extract to a boil. Temper in egg yolks and cornstarch, cooking until thickened. Remove from heat and stir in butter. Allow to cool overnight.

Jaconde (Almond Sponge Cake)
3 cups + 2 tbsp. almond paste (one part almond, one part sugar)
5 tbsp. butter
8 (2 cups) whole eggs
3¾ cups all-purpose flour
1 tbsp. cocoa powder
11 egg whites
½ cup sugar

Cream almond paste and butter well. Add whole eggs and beat with an electric mixer 8-10 minutes. Fold in flour and cocoa powder. In a separate bowl, whip whites and sugar to medium peak; fold into almond paste mixture. Spread on silicone baking mat on full sheet pan and bake 325 degrees for 10-12 minutes. Allow to cool.

Divide Toasted Almond Cream into two parts. Spread half on Jaconde and roll tightly; freeze for 1 hour. When set, cut off end pieces and place them decoratively to mimic a cut log. Roughly spread remaining cream over the log as icing. Garnish as desired with festive accents.

Yields 10 servings.

Tariq Hanna is executive chef and co-owner of the popular Sucré, which serves fancy desserts and sweets. He prepares the traditional bûche de Noël *dessert during the Christmas season. (Photo by Peggy Scott Laborde)*

Local navel oranges are used in this fruitcake prepared by Maureen Reed Detweiler.
(Photo by Peggy Scott Laborde)

Louisiana Navel Orange Fruitcake

Maureen Reed Detweiler

New Orleans culinary enthusiast and nationally recognized antique rose expert Maureen Reed Detweiler shares her Grandmother Reed's recipe. "She made the cakes every year when Louisiana navel oranges were in season," says Detweiler, "and now I make them."

New Orleans culinary enthusiast Maureen Reed Detweiler encourages the use of local ingredients in her fruitcake recipe. (Photo by Peggy Scott Laborde)

4 Louisiana navel oranges
1 cup butter
2 cups sugar
4 eggs
½ cup buttermilk
3½ cups all-purpose flour
1 tsp. baking soda
1 cup pecan pieces
1 cup chopped dates
2 cups powdered sugar
2 tbsp. fine dark rum

Finely grate the peel of the 4 oranges to create 4 tbsp. of zest. Set aside. Squeeze the juice from the oranges to make 1 cup. Set aside.

Cream butter with sugar. Add eggs and buttermilk. Beat well. Add 2 tbsp. of the reserved orange peel, flour, and baking soda, beating mixture until smooth. Add pecan pieces and chopped dates. Mix well. Butter a stem pan or bundt and line it with buttered brown paper. Pour batter into pan and bake 1 hour and 45 minutes at 275 degrees.

While cake is baking, mix powdered sugar, 1 cup reserved orange juice, 2 tbsp. reserved orange peel, and rum in a small pitcher or bowl. As soon as cake is removed from oven, pour half of the orange juice mixture over cake in the pan. It will soak into the hot cake. Allow cake to cool for 30 minutes. Turn cake out upside down on a plate. Slowly pour the remaining orange juice mixture over cake, puncturing it with the tines of a fork so that it will soak into cake. Cover cake with plastic wrap or foil and chill.

Yields 16 servings.

New Orleans native Chris Yacich wrote the Christmas song "That's What I Wrote to Santa Claus," published nationally in 1939. (The Historic New Orleans Collection)

CHAPTER NINE

New Orleans Christmas in Music, Verse, and Art

A Musical Heritage

Musical celebration has been part of New Orleans since its inception. The original settlers turned to music for respite and escape during those first difficult days. Clearing land for a brand-new settlement in a humid place where mosquitoes were part of the scenery had been exhausting. By Christmas 1718 there were four buildings, and a lot of hope for this venture, but the men were worn out and cold. The twenty-fifth of December was a day for rest, savoring the turkeys that had been plucked from the woods and roasted, and sipping a recent delivery of wine and brandy from the motherland. Part of the festivity included singing songs—carols that had been sung for ages, sweet reminders of home—in the mother tongue, French. And there was probably dancing, mostly in a circle. It was New Orleans' first Christmas.

France has had a long tradition of Christmas music. The French word *carole* means a song that originally accompanied a festive circle dance. Carols based on scriptures were forbidden since church Christmas music tended to be dark, somber, and Latin. Joyful Christmas melodies were more secular, and at the start of the 1700s these songs tended to be performed as gavottes (a lively circle dance that includes skipping steps) and minuets. Some songs were ribald since Christmas then was a rather boisterous occasion.

Christmas Music in Nineteenth-Century New Orleans

Most of the Christmas carols we know today were not introduced until the nineteenth century, and it is Britain that provided such early pre-nineteenth century standards as "God Rest Ye Merry, Gentlemen" and "Deck the Halls." Davies Gilbert's *Some Ancient Carols, with the Tunes to Which They Were Formerly Sung in the West of England*, published in 1822, and more importantly William B. Sandys' *Christmas Carols Ancient and Modern*, published in 1833, helped bring British Christmas carols out of the shadows not only in Britain but also in the United States. Old British carols were soon joined by American carols including "We Three Kings" and "It Came Upon a Midnight Clear."

In its 1865 Christmas edition, the *Daily Picayune* mentioned local

Best New Orleans Christmas Music

In addition to the traditional carols and classical music associated with the Christmas season, it can hardly be a surprise that there are Christmas CDs featuring New Orleans jazz and R&B musicians. We asked New Orleans music radio station WWOZ producer/announcer Jim Hobbs for a list of his favorite holiday albums.

Christmas is both a sacred and a secular celebration. In the same vein, New Orleans Christmas music is somber and moving, and it can also be joyful and playful, even comic. Holiday music is found in every genre, from traditional to modern jazz, from gospel to rhythm-and-blues. Here are some of the best local holiday recordings:

Johnny Adams. *Christmas in New Orleans*. Mardi Gras, 1994. The "Tan Canary" pours out his brand of honeyed vocals on this collection of holiday standards, from the religious "Silent Night" to the secular "White Christmas." A competent band, with a measured beat and approach, supports his soulful singing.

Louis Armstrong. *The Best of Louis Armstrong & Friends: The Christmas Collection*. Hip-O Records, 2003. This disk is only half Armstrong, the remainder filled with other classics like Eartha Kitt's "Santa Baby." But it's too good to pass up, with Armstrong's best Christmas songs, "Zat You, Santa Claus?", "Cool Yule," and "Christmas in New Orleans." "Zat You"

The seventh selection on the front page of this book of sheet music is "Cantique de Noël," a universally renowned nineteenth-century French Christmas carol that would have been sung in New Orleans. Its English lyrics are not a translation of the original but are known as the equally beloved "O Holy Night." (The Historic New Orleans Collection)

recognition and popularity of English carols in an editorial observing the end of the Civil War and the reuniting of family ties. The newspaper hoped families would sing: "Hark the herald angels sing / Glory to the new born King, / Peace on Earth, and mercy mild, / God and sinners reconciled."

As Christmas's then traditional rowdiness was being increasingly held in disdain, the nineteenth-century middle classes embraced a growing solemnity, grandeur, and pomposity to the season's music. This was especially true in the churches. A carol most symbolic of the Victorian status of Christmas in Creole New Orleans was "Cantique de Noël," composed by Adolphe Adam in 1847 to the poem "Minuit Crétiens" by Placide Cappeau. With the same tune but different lyrics, it is popularly known in English as "O Holy Night."

In New Orleans, Christmas Eve church programs often went on for hours, while in larger Catholic churches there were multiple Christmas Day masses, each mass often presenting a different selection of music. On Christmas morning, newspapers listed all of the churches and the day's planned musical performances; the next day they reviewed the performances as if they were theater productions.

In 1875 the *Daily Picayune* extolled the quality of the choir and

Santa Claus' Music Satchel is an 1868 collection of melodies published by A. E. Blackmar in New Orleans. (From the collection of Justin deGrange Winston)

presentation at St. Anne's Roman Catholic Church, commenting that the performance "in this church . . . on account of its grandeur and solemnity, was perhaps not excelled by any other church in the city." At the Church of the Immaculate Conception the choir was praised for its Christmas Eve rendition in "exquisite taste" of Adam's "Cantique de Noël," which was followed by Gounod's Grand Mass. The next morning there was a performance of Von Weber's Solemn Mass in E.

In 1880, of Christ Church the *Picayune* wrote, "The music at this place of worship is always noticeable for its sacred character and appropriateness. . . . The 'Hallelujah Chorus' from Handel's 'Messiah' had been selected for the opening piece [and] was sung with great spirit." St. Anna's, another Episcopal church, was famous for its Christmas Eve Communion service, which could go on for hours with various musical performances. In 1900 the *Picayune* said that the service was "interspersed with the numbers of a most beautiful musical programme . . . the choir, assisted by a number of distinguished vocalists. The effect was grand . . . one of the most beautiful Christmas ceremonies of the season."

Christmas had its share of light secular music in the nineteenth century. *Santa Claus' Music Satchel,* a collection of lively tunes for the holidays, was published in 1868 by Blackmar, the Canal Street music publisher. The South's own E. O. Eaton, composer of the "Orleans Cadet Quickstep," wrote a Christmas number called "Merry Christmas," which was published in 1874, also by Blackmar.

is full of humor, urging Santa to slip his present under the door. It's also been recorded by such a diverse group as local chanteuses Ingrid Lucia and Banu Gibson, Brian Setzer, Buster Poindexter, Bing Crosby, the Asylum Street Spankers, and even the Muppets. "Christmas in New Orleans" is a nostalgic look at the Crescent City's holiday, with sights such as a "Dixieland Santa Claus leading the band to a good old Creole beat." "Cool Yule" doesn't even mention New Orleans, but just the voice and style have "New Orleans" written all over them.

Benny Grunch and the Bunch. *The 12 Yats of Christmas.* Benjie Records, 2007. Benny Grunch Antin is the local comic king of Christmas with the perennial favorite, "The 12 Yats of Christmas," which is squarely in the humorous category. It's overflowing with New Orleans versions of old favorites and entirely original songs such as "Santa and His Reindeer Used to

Songwriter and bandleader Benny Grunch's "The 12 Yats of Christmas" features landmarks and references unique to New Orleans. Grunch's devotion to the city's more recent past is reflected in his original songs, which include "Ain't Dere No More." (Photo by Peggy Scott Laborde)

Live Right Here" and the got-to-laugh-to-keep-from-crying "I'm Dreaming of a White Trailer." Grunch expands it every year; it's now up to two disks (Side K and Side B) and comes complete with sing-along versions of many songs. Also includes lyrics.

Aaron Neville. *Aaron Neville's Soulful Christmas*. A&M Records, 1993. No Christmas is complete at my house without this collection of standards. Aaron's smooth voice glides through the religious "O Holy Night" and "O Little Town of Bethlehem." "Please Come Home for Christmas" is full of plaintive longing, and the zydeco-flavored "Louisiana Christmas Day" is a treat.

Allen Toussaint and Friends. *A New Orleans Christmas*. NYRO, 1997. A variety of artists performing individually rather than as an ensemble. Toussaint plies his piano magic on "Silent Night, Holy Night" and "Winter Wonderland." New Birth Brass Band's "Santa's Second Line" is a rollicking second line and "Christmas in New Orleans" is by James Andrews. There was never a funkier "Do You Hear What I Hear?" than the one by Tricia Boutte.

Vince Vance and the Valiants. *All I Want for Christmas Is You*. Waldoxy, 1992. No New Orleans Christmas party (for two or more) is complete without the song "All I Want for Christmas Is You." The vocal performance is full of energy and longing, the saxophone solo swinging and uplifting, all beautifully

A. E. Blackmar in New Orleans published a Christmas carol titled "Merry Christmas" in 1874. (The Historic New Orleans Collection)

Twentieth-Century Tunes

Around the turn of the twentieth century, small salon orchestras usually provided music at local hotels and restaurants. James A. Meade's orchestra played for the St. Charles Hotel Christmas dinner of 1909. The only Christmas offerings were a march called "Merry Xmas" by Meade himself and another simply titled "Santa Claus" by "Vokoum." Other numbers were light classic selections from Bizet's *Carmen*, Suppe's *Pique Dame*, Brahms' *Hungarian Dances*, and *Tales of Hoffman* by Offenbach.

In New Orleans, as well as across America, there was Christmas caroling in the streets. With the United States' entry into World War I, large crowds gathered in Lafayette Square in community-sponsored caroling, and after World War II the Patio Planters began organizing caroling in Jackson Square, which thousands of people attend each year.

Pat Duvall's "Little Christmas Tree" was published by the French Quarter Music Company of New Orleans in 1964. (The Historic New Orleans Collection)

With the rise of the twentieth century, popular culture was fed first by the phonograph then radio, films, and television. Secular Christmas carols grew to dominate the season. Haven Gillespie and Fred Coots' "Santa Claus Is Coming to Town" and Irving Berlin's "White Christmas" were both first sung to Americans on the radio in 1934 and 1941, respectively. Baby boomers everywhere—including those in New Orleans and its burgeoning 1950s suburbs—were captivated when they first heard cowboy crooner Gene Autry sing Johnny Marks' "Rudolph the Red-Nosed Reindeer" in 1949 and Steve Nelson and Jack Rollins' "Frosty the Snowman" in 1951. There were also Katherine Kennicott Davis's "Little Drummer Boy" in 1959 and Noel Regney and Gloria Shayne's "Do You Hear What I Hear?" from 1962 to bring nostalgia to the post-World War II generation.

In New Orleans, in 1939 there was "That's What I Wrote to Santa Claus" by Chris Yacich. It tells the story of a person asking Santa for a

recorded. The disk is filled out with half classics and half original songs.

Various Artists. *Putumayo Presents: New Orleans Christmas.* Putumayo, 2006. This is a wide-ranging collection spanning brass band to traditional jazz to modern jazz, all with a swinging beat. Big Al Carson does the vocals with Lars Edegran and His Santa Claus Revelers on "Santa Claus Is Comin' to Town," a great traditional jazz romp, with clarinet and trombone solos. You'll be strutting with some candy canes on "Christmas in New Orleans," "Silver Bells," and "Santa's Second Line." Settle back for some ear-caressing vocals from Ingrid Lucia, Banu Gibson, and Topsy Chapman.

Jim Hobbs is a volunteer engineer and programmer with radio station WWOZ-FM 90.7 New Orleans. He has published articles on music and CD reviews and is also compiling a complete list of Cajun, Louisiana Creole, and zydeco recordings. Jim's Christmas wish is enough time to dance to all the good music in the world (and peace on earth).

Deacon John's Christmas Memories

New Orleans R&B guitarist/ singer/bandleader "Deacon John" Moore has been a part of the local music scene since the 1960s. Moore grew up in a very devout Catholic family that included thirteen children. His neighborhood was the predominantly black Creole Seventh Ward. He attended Corpus Christi Grammar School and has vivid Christmas memories.

Q: What did Christmas mean to you as a child?

A: It meant a lot of presents. It meant a lot of work for my mother, you know, because we all had to go to mass and Communion. Of course I sang in the boys' choir. I had to do Midnight Mass and all the Lenten church services. My mother, being such a devout Catholic, had a tradition of staging a Christmas pageant in our home. As the children became more numerous, we had a whole cast of characters for the Nativity scene. We had angels, shepherds, wise men, Virgin Mary and Saint Joseph, and we had a new baby Jesus almost every year. We'd have a brand-new baby Jesus!

"Deacon John" Moore, center, sings in the boys' choir of Corpus Christi Church in the early 1950s. (Courtesy of "Deacon John" Moore)

Popular New Orleans singer Al Carson is featured in the album Crescent City Christmas *by Lars Edegran and His Santa Claus Revelers. The group can also be heard on the* Putumayo Presents: New Orleans Christmas *album. (Courtesy of Judy Cooper)*

true and dependable friend. Although the song was published nationally by the Clarence Williams Music Publishing Company and is not about New Orleans, composer Yacich grew up in the area and was on the staff of WWL Radio. He wrote material for the phenomenally popular *Dawnbusters* program. He was also nationally known for the song "I Like Bananas (Because They Have No Bones)", which was recorded by the Hoosier Hot Shots and Kay Kyser. Yacich was also a silent collaborator in writing Huey Long's theme song, "Every Man a King."

Richard Sherman and Joe Van Winkle's "Christmas in New Orleans" is made magical by Louis Armstrong's 1952 version, but it's hard not to giggle upon hearing lyrics such as "Magnolia trees at night, sparkling bright, fields of cotton looking wintery white."

In 1964 the French Quarter Music Company published Pat DuVall's "Little Christmas Tree." In it DuVall sings of a twinkling tree that in the style of the 1960s must be on a turntable, since it goes round and round "like a ballerina on her toes."

In the late 1980s the New Orleans band Vince Vance and the Valiants had a hit, "All I Want for Christmas Is You."

Since the mid-1990s, more notable for local Christmas nostalgia is "The 12 Yats of Christmas," a humorous parody of local traditions naming an assortment of New Orleans-related items such as crawfish and Dixie Beer. Written by Benny Grunch Antin, it parodies "The Twelve Days of Christmas" in a city where the Twelve Days and Twelfth Night have a bit more meaning than elsewhere. Other songs in Grunch's catalogue include "O Little Town of Destrehan."

While there are enough Christmas albums by New Orleans musicians to fill Santa's sack many times over, especially notable is singer/banjo player Banu Gibson and her Hot New Orleans Jazz Band's delightful "Zat You, Santa Claus?", and "Crescent City Christmas" by Lars Edegran and His Santa Claus Revelers. A real treat on this recording are the vocals by Big Al Carson and the album cover itself, with the singer dressed as Santa. Singers Topsy Chapman and Dwayne Burns also contribute their talents.

Season's Readings

The image of Santa in muskrat from head to toe and with a skiff pulled by alligators began in the 1970s as a Christmas greeting for a local car dealership. Howard Jacobs, who had been a columnist for the *Times-Picayune,* wrote the original storyline under the pen name "Trosclair." With illustrations by James Rice, local publisher Pelican Publishing Company turned the poem into a modern-day classic, *Cajun Night Before Christmas*®.

The first of more than sixty books illustrated or penned by the Texas-born Rice, *Cajun Night Before Christmas*® launched Pelican's successful series of illustrated books parodying the Christmas traditions of various places and peoples. Nearly a million copies of the Cajun twist on *The Night Before Christmas* are in print, and each year when Christmas books with a regional flavor pop up in local bookstores, the late artist/author James Rice's *Cajun Night Before Christmas*® is among them.

On shelves alongside the humorous tale of Christmas on the bayou, a gingerbread boy's adventures in Cajun country appear. The *Cajun Gingerbread Boy*, by New Orleans children's book author Berthe Amoss, follows the Christmas cookie as he keeps one step ahead of such characters as Mawmaw, the shrimper, the fiddler, the farmer, and M'sieur Cocodrie, the alligator. With these and other locally themed stories, Christmas readings in New Orleans are entertaining for children of all ages.

My mother had an arsenal of old clothing because we lived on hand-me-downs. Clothes were donated to us by the religious community, particularly the nuns and the priests. So my mother would take old robes and she'd dress me up like Saint Joseph in a robe, with a cane like a staff. And she always had a nice gown for the Blessed Mother. One of my sisters would be Blessed Mother. And they'd take turns: "You are the Blessed Mother this year. Next year you be the Blessed Mother. No, I want to be Saint Joseph. No, you be one of the angels this year." And everybody wanted to be one of the angels or the shepherds because those were the non-speaking parts. We'd just stand there and we could make faces and make anybody laugh while they were trying to recite their lines!

We went through the whole recitation of the biblical story. And my mother had a script written out and we all had parts. We'd put on a Christmas play for my mother and her friends and relatives and the people in the neighborhood. The nuns and priests at school would come over to see the play.

Under his mother's direction, "Deacon John" Moore, shown wearing a tie and sweater, and his family staged an annual Christmas pageant for friends and neighbors. (Courtesy of "Deacon John" Moore)

New Orleans rhythm-and-blues legend "Deacon John" Moore. (Photo by Peggy Scott Laborde)

Q: Where did your Christmas presents come from?

A: Presents. Well, fortunately, my mother, being the saintly person that she was, she knew a lot of nuns who would give us surplus foods and candy they would get from the various charities. And we would get candy from different candy companies that would donate to the nuns and the schools, so they would pass them on down to my mother. We had plenty of candy and we also would get presents from the relatives of the nuns.

Q: Tell me about getting your picture taken with Santa.

A: We would go down to take pictures with Santa Claus at Maison Blanche. Oh, the first time I didn't like it. I didn't like Santa Claus. I was scared of him. [Laughs] I was scared. I said, "Who's this white dude?" They didn't have black Santa Clauses then; they were all white. [Laughing] I was scared of him.

Q: Were there any favorite Christmas dishes on the dinner table?

A: Every Christmas we had a

Over a half-million copies of Cajun Night Before Christmas® *by James Rice have been sold. The story of Santa pulling a sleigh of alligators has become a beloved tale that spawned a series of books. (Courtesy of Pelican Publishing Company)*

O Holy Light

The Nativity captures the essence of the Christmas message, and one of the most beautiful ways of conveying the "reason for the season" is through stained glass. While scenes from the life of Christ abound in local houses of worship, Christmas is the perfect time to look up and take notice of an artisan's work that has endured for all of us to seek and find inspiration.

Since its namesake is a member of the Holy Family, it's only fitting that St. Joseph Roman Catholic Church, 1802 Tulane Avenue, has a Nativity window. This church opened in 1893 following a growth spurt that necessitated a bigger structure for the then almost half-century-old parish. With a seating capacity of two thousand, St. Joseph's is one of the largest churches in New Orleans and popular with brides for its 150-foot-long aisle.

At the Episcopal Christ Church Cathedral, 2919 St. Charles Avenue, the message of Christ's birth is illustrated in glass in a window spanning the front of the English Gothic-style house of worship. The

Around New Orleans many churches feature Nativity scenes in stained glass. This one is from St. Joseph's on Tulane Avenue. (Photo by Peggy Scott Laborde)

turkey 'cause my father would buy the turkeys when they were small. He'd go to the French Market and he'd feel the breasts to get ones that were still developing. And a year later he would have a really big turkey. I remember one Thanksgiving my father had a thirty-five-pound turkey. He raised a thirty-five-pound turkey and we were scared to go in the yard because the turkey would see us come in the yard and he would run after us.

Q. Christmas Eve memories?

A. After Midnight Mass, we'd come home and go sneak and look at the presents and start eating the fruit from the Christmas stockings and the candy. We'd have an early start because we'd go to Midnight Mass and the other kids would be still asleep when we got back home so we had first pick at the candy. Of course there was tons of candy because the religious community just bent over backwards to help my mother. . . . So we never had to want for Christmas. We didn't have money to go out and buy presents, except maybe for the little dime store variety to exchange among ourselves. But for the most part we got candy and presents donated by the religious community. And clothing too 'cause all of a sudden, you know, you'd get a brand-new overcoat, a pea coat, you know, like the military wore. Mom would say, "Okay that one's for you. That's your size. Next year you've got to give it to John when he grows into it."

Q. How about Christmas dinner and other preparations?

A. Christmas preparations were gargantuan tasks for my mother, and so we all had to pitch in to help her. As far as the cooking, my sisters helped my mother prepare the turkeys and the pies, the mincemeat pies, the pumpkin pies, and the apple pies. And then there was the gumbo, which took a long time to prepare. My sisters would chop up the ingredients and all to help my mother cook the gumbo. And then there was the sweet potato pie. And then there was, you know, the sweet potatoes and all the vegetables, the corn on the cob. And so to prepare this big feast it took a whole day in preparation.

There was all the preparing of the stockings and putting the fruit and the nuts in the stockings and then wrapping the presents with all the toys and the clothes and the making the Christmas cards because we had tons of relatives to send Christmas cards out to. And then there were all the nuns and the priests and the friends of my mother. My mother had a huge Christmas card mailing list.

Then there was the preparation of the annual Christmas tree. We had to go out and get the Christmas tree. My father would take a bucket and fill it up with bricks and dirt and position the tree inside the bucket and make his own stand so he wouldn't have to buy one. And every year we had to prepare the tree, and of course there was decorating the tree. And my mother had the Nativity scene under the tree and she had some really old figurines, like of St. Joseph and the Virgin Mary, and she had the shepherds and the

Light shining through the tint of blue encompassing this work of art highlights the craftsmanship of the artisans who created the windows for St. John the Baptist Catholic church. (Photo by Frank Methe)

triptych depicts the visit of the Wise Men on one side of the Holy Family and the shepherds on the other. This is a stunning, "bathed in blue" depiction of the ultimate message of hope. The windows were created by the Burnham Company of Boston, its employees German immigrants.

In what is today's Irish Channel stands a majestic German Baroque edifice called St. Mary's Assumption Church, 2030 Constance Street, serving St. Alphonsus Parish. It was constructed in 1858. This neighborhood was once a mix of Irish, German, and French immigrants, each adamant about having their own church. While the French church is no more, the Irish St. Alphonsus has been turned into a cultural arts center and the German St. Mary's now stands as the lone house of worship in a mostly poor neighborhood. In 1866, the Bavarian-born Redemptorist priest Francis Xavier Seelos was assigned to St. Mary's, ultimately losing his own life the next year while caring for his congregation during a yellow fever epidemic. Behind the church his remains are housed in an elegant reliquary located in a small shrine/museum that serves as the international headquarters for efforts promoting Seelos's canonization. Over the years numerous

Wise Men, animals, and her stable. All that had to be assembled every year and you had to take great caution not to break any of the old stuff that was passed down from generation to generation. I still have some of the little figurines that my mother passed down to us.

Q: You mentioned earlier you were in the church choir.

A: My mother put me in the choir because she said I cried the loudest out of all her thirteen children so she thought I would have a singing voice. Well, she was right. I did have the loudest voice in the choir so consequently they would give me a lot of solos. And at Midnight Mass, I would sing "O Holy Night." And my mother would be so proud. She'd look up in the choir loft and see her son singing. Well, one particular Christmas Eve, I drank some of my father's wine before I went to Midnight Mass. And my mother said she never heard me sing so beautifully!

Located in the choir loft of St. Mary's Assumption, this detail of a Nativity scene made in the 1800s may be fading but is nevertheless touching. (Photo by Peggy Scott Laborde)

miracles have been attributed to the intercession of the priest and he is on the path to sainthood.

The windows of St. Mary's Assumption were made by German artisans, pioneers in stained glass. On view is St. Nicholas of Myra, the precursor to St. Nick. He can been seen saving three children who are in a tub below him and is considered the patron saint of children.

Up in the choir loft, alas hidden to most of the faithful attending church services, is a Nativity imported from Germany and of the Munich school of stained-glass design. In a mostly dark brown hue, but still visible is the Holy Family; however, a fading baby Jesus is close to being overwhelmed by light. This window is one of the few transferred from the original smaller 1844 church that originally stood on the site. The chances are very good that Father Seelos himself admired this Christmas masterpiece.

St. George's Episcopal Church, 4600 St. Charles Avenue, opened for services in 1900. Its Nativity window was made by the New York-based Tiffany Glass Company. The hues of blue in the sky and in Mary's cloak make this artwork a true standout.

As December approaches, consider taking your own tour of stained-glass gems. Look up above the altar and catch some of that holy light.

CHAPTER TEN

A Katrina Christmas

The Christmas following the catastrophe of Hurricane Katrina on August 29, 2005, will never be forgotten by locals. Attempts at celebrating the holiday season were viewed as one step towards recovery.

December 2005 came less than four months after the failure of some of the city's levees, causing the loss of nearly two thousand lives and the devastation of three hundred thousand homes, along with the forced evacuation of the entire city, a disaster whose magnitude was unheard of in American history. New Orleans started repopulating in early October. While east Jefferson Parish and Westbank suburbs had regained most of their population by December 2005, the city proper contained barely 100,000 of its pre-storm population of 485,000. Many families remained scattered from one end of the country to the other.

In late November the *Times-Picayune* headlined that it would be "A Very Different Christmas." Individuals interviewed by the newspaper said that they found it difficult to celebrate and were not into the spirit of the season. For some folks, however, Christmas was the first real breather after not only the horrors of Katrina, but also an unusually active hurricane season that sent three hurricanes toward the Louisiana coast (Cindy, Katrina, and Rita). Not until December did the season show signs of winding down.

New Orleanians celebrated Christmas as best as they could, and popular *Times-Picayune* columnist Chris Rose perhaps best summed up local feelings when he wrote: "Sure, you can slow us down, pare our ranks, tear at our foundations until we cry for mercy. But YOU CAN'T STOP US."

There was little, if any postal service so the sending of Christmas cards was something to scratch off the list. Even with lack of service, many locals weren't at home to receive cards—most were in temporary shelters while they renovated. The media ran stories about the mental health of the community during a post-Katrina Christmas, and children wrote letters to Santa Claus asking him for help in putting their houses back together.

Lighting displays were not as bright as in years past, but fortunately some whimsy prevailed. As many people struggled with paperwork to get into FEMA trailers, others already in their temporary residences decorated them with strings of lights and greenery. A few people

Leah Chase's Katrina Christmas

Leah Chase, who, together with her husband, owns Dooky Chase, one of the city's oldest Creole restaurants, is a beloved civic activist and collector of works by African-American artists. The couple's home and the restaurant were severely damaged by the flooding after Hurricane Katrina. The restaurant is now restored and the Chases, both in their eighties, are working hard to continue their business, which is more than half a century old. Chase recalls her "Katrina Christmas" in a 2006 interview for WYES-TV.

Katrina came and we thought, "Oh, it's going away, and we'll be back home and we'll have Thanksgiving and Christmas" but that did not happen. So here we are in a house in Baton Rouge, with about fifteen people in a three-bedroom house and a good kitchen though. So we had to have Christmas. You have to have those things. Nothing can take that away. You can't pass Christmas. That's a big day. You can't have that go away without anything. So we had good people—they brought a Christmas tablecloth, candles, Christmas everything—and I cooked gumbo and did all of our Christmas things on Christmas Day. People gave us a lot. We had a two-foot Christmas tree but it was fun. We had Christmas and we were together. About twenty-five to eat in that house. So Christmas was great. Christmas was good. You make Christmas and you do festive things and you have gifts, it could be little things, but we had bags of gifts for the children, for everybody.

Even though many people in the New Orleans area were living in temporary housing after Hurricane Katrina, they still showed their Christmas spirit by decorating. (Courtesy of WYES-TV)

hung wreaths on the doors of their ruined homes. Lights were strung on a few ragged stumps of trees felled by the storm. Because of the lengthy power outage in most of the city post-Katrina, a common sight was refrigerators taped shut and full of rotted food left on curbs to be picked up by FEMA-hired clean-up crews. As the holidays approached, several refrigerators were spotted adorned with sets of lights and wreaths.

As soon as some restaurants reopened in October, their reservations desks were inundated with callers seeking tables for Christmas Eve and holiday *réveillon* dinners. After all of the change in so many people's lives, the yearning for normalcy was strong. Restaurant owners found their tables were more filled than usual since families without a roof over their heads also lacked kitchens.

While most of the Christmas lights around New Orleans were doused for the year, one beloved tradition, Celebration in the Oaks, went on as usual, although reduced in size. Its surroundings in City Park had been inundated and many of the park's trees were shattered skeletons. Streets and houses remained dark and lifeless in the nearby neighborhoods of Lakeview and Gentilly, which had been drained of floodwater only three months earlier. Yet Celebration held its kick-off party in early December, to the relief of people who yearned for a normal Christmas.

Christmas Shopping after Katrina

The city's Christmas shopping season was thrown off kilter by the storm. Even for those families that didn't lose everything, 2005 was

"Buy local" was a mantra during the Christmas season after Hurricane Katrina. The fleur-de-lis, a symbol of New Orleans, was especially popular. (Photo by Peggy Scott Laborde)

What Happened to Mr. Bingle? (His Katrina Story)

Videographer Jeff Kent was a protégé of the puppeteer Oscar Isentrout, the creator of the Mr. Bingle marionette. Kent now owns the Mr. Bingle that starred in the popular Maison Blanche window shows that took place during the Christmas season from the late 1940s through the early 1980s. As with so many New Orleanians, Kent's home was destroyed when the levees failed after Hurricane Katrina. In this interview Kent chronicles his efforts to bring back Bingle.

It was several days after Katrina when I finally got out of New Orleans, and I realized I had probably lost everything I owned. My feeling was it could all be replaced and I wasn't too concerned. It was when I arrived at my sister's house in Kingsport, Tennessee, that I remembered that Bingle was still in a closet in my home. Actually, my concern was that someone would steal him. You see, I really don't feel I own the Mr. Bingle marionette; I'm more like his caretaker, for he really belongs to everyone. My desire to return home had suddenly become desperate.

I acquired the marionette from a Maison Blanche department store employee after Oscar [Isentrout] died in 1985. There was one other Bingle puppet who was mostly a rod puppet. It was also converted into a marionette at times. It can be identified by its oversized head. The one I have with a smaller head is the one that played in the window shows, on television, and is the one I used in the traveling shows back in the early '80s.

Santa's Quarters is just one of many shops that features fleur-de-lis merchandise since Hurricane Katrina. (Photo by Peggy Scott Laborde)

a difficult holiday season for a community that was traumatized by loss. Late-night Christmas shopping was curtailed, as stores were open shorter hours due to a severe labor shortage. Shipments were delayed, leaving stock low. Toy stores were left in a lurch since there were few children living in the city. Along with their families, most had not returned from evacuation and were enrolled in out-of-town schools.

Katrina damaged many shopping centers. The huge Plaza Mall at Lake Forest and New Orleans Centre downtown closed, never to reopen. On the Westbank the Oakwood Mall, while not flooded, had been heavily looted and burned in the storm's aftermath; it didn't reopen until Christmas 2007. Popular shopping areas such as Harrison Avenue in Lakeview and Gentilly Woods in Gentilly had been heavily flooded.

Downtown the luxurious Shops at Canal Place, with anchors such as Saks Fifth Avenue and Brooks Brothers, was closed and did not reopen until after Christmas. Saks, which was looted and burned after the storm, reopened just before Christmas 2006 considerably expanded and redecorated. The Riverwalk Marketplace was open for Christmas 2005, but at the time many of its shops were still shuttered and the aisles of the old wharf-turned-mall remained eerily quiet. On Canal Street the luxury clothier Rubensteins suffered only minor flooding and was able to reopen in mid-October after being spared any looting since the police marshalling center after Katrina was next to the store. The jeweler Adler's experienced looting and flooding but reopened in time for Christmas.

Magazine Street has evolved into one of the city's trendiest shopping districts, with almost six miles of boutiques and other businesses. The long street emerged from the storm virtually unscathed, except for some looting, and was entirely untouched by floodwaters. It was the heart of the unflooded, relatively high uptown area within a mile of the Mississippi River that was dubbed the "sliver by the river." Magazine Street was an oasis and gave hope in a city where so much was damaged. Its dress boutiques, gift stores, and antique shops began reopening in early October, when residents were allowed to return to the city. At Christmas many of its shops benefited; for a while Magazine became *the* main shopping street within city limits. The very sight of Christmas shoppers on Magazine Street carrying shopping bags could lift spirits and represented a step towards the goal of feeling that a part of the city was getting back to normal, though nothing was really normal.

Shoppers focused on buying locally. It was a matter of the utmost importance and a point of civic pride to shop at home. For some this meant shopping on Magazine Street, since sales tax would go to the city. New Orleanians who were still living out of town returned to spend their Christmas money at home, and out-of-town visitors felt they were doing a good deed by spending their holiday dollars in New Orleans.

Distinctly New Orleans items became wildly popular for holiday gifts and would remain so for some time. Anything fleur-de-lis—the symbol of the city and its revival—was especially sought after. There were also magnets, trivets, and other items based on the city's distinctive Sewerage and Water Board meter covers. The Mr. Bingle doll, that symbol of New Orleans Christmas, was more popular than ever. Reproductions of recent front pages and photographs from the *Times-Picayune* were likewise considered appropriate gifts. Indeed, rings, mugs, jewelry—anything from or about New Orleans—turned out to be hot sellers.

Display Controversy in Metairie

With so many other malls and shopping areas damaged by Hurricane Katrina and its aftermath, suburban malls such as Lakeside in Metairie and the Esplanade in Kenner reopened and experienced a sharp increase in traffic. For shoppers on the Westbank, where Oakwood was temporarily out of commission, Lakeside provided shuttle buses.

Along with the increased foot traffic at Lakeside came a Christmastime controversy when a well-meant tongue-in-cheek, yet to some people offensive, holiday display was installed at the center of the mall. Landscape architect Frank Evans, who for thirteen years had constructed Lakeside's Christmas village display, added a few touches to reflect New Orleans post-Katrina. He put small blue tarps on the roofs of many of the miniature homes. The addition very much reflected the cityscape that was filled with wind-damaged roofs covered with blue FEMA-provided tarpaulins. In front of some

Q: What condition did you find him in?

A: A month after Katrina, I returned to New Orleans, and when I got to my house I actually videotaped my finding him. Before the storm he was hanging in a closet in my home. I found him upside down on his head on the floor of the closet. Bingle was fully intact. Laying in salt water for nearly a month created rust stains on his "bunny suit"—Oscar used to call it that; it's the fur costume that goes over the body—as well as the wooden body underneath his suit. The only major concern I had was his snow-cone hat. The hat was bent and softened from being wet. Residue from the dirty water stained his eyes and the mouth was not working.

The original Mr. Bingle puppet that danced in the Canal Street window of Maison Blanche department store for so many years was damaged in Hurricane Katrina but later restored by puppeteer Jeff Kent. (Courtesy of Jeff Kent)

Puppeteer Jeff Kent carefully restored the beloved symbol of New Orleans Christmas. (Courtesy of Jeff Kent)

Q: When did you refurbish him?

A: While working at WVUE-TV Fox 8, I showed pictures of Bingle to Bob Breck. Bob encouraged me to fix up Bingle. In the first week of December 2005, the two of us decided to document the process by creating a news story on Bingle's restoration. It took about a week.

Q: Describe the process.

A: The most important thing I wanted to do was preserve as many of Bingle's original parts as possible. I first took the puppet apart and found that nearly all of the metal parts were damaged by the salt water and replaced them. These were screw eyes, nails, and rods. I sanded off all of the rust. There is a mechanism in the head that uses a piece of elastic that acts like a spring that keeps Bingle's mouth closed. When a string is pulled to open it, the elastic moves the mouth back in place when the string is released. This was replaced. The body underneath the suit was repainted. I actually had to purchase a new sewing machine to sew the bunny suit and gloves. I found a fur different from what

In 2005, Lakeside Shopping Center's Christmas village reflected the reality of the first post-Katrina Christmas season with tiny cottages sporting blue tarpaulins on damaged roofs. (Photo by Peggy Scott Laborde)

This cottage at Lakeside Shopping Center's Christmas village displays a blue tarpaulin and a miniature refrigerator posted, "You Loot/We Shoot." (Photo by Peggy Scott Laborde)

of the houses, tiny abandoned refrigerators sat on the streets. There was even a scene of a flood victim climbing a rope suspended from a helicopter. A miniature pumping station labeled "Broussard Pumping Station No. 1—Works only in good weather" lampooned Jefferson Parish president Aaron Broussard for allowing the evacuation of parish pump operators, resulting in flooding in Jefferson Parish.

The display was amusing to many, but it hit a bit too close to home in time and spirit for some, who complained to the mall's management. Lakeside's management apologized to "those customers who were offended." Some aspects were removed but the display still reflected the times. There were shoppers who actually voiced dismay that the original display had been modified.

Katrina Humor

Humor and a momentary good laugh or smile helped in some people's emotional recovery from the shock of Katrina. Jokes about refrigerators filled with rotting food and mold spores filling the air abounded and allowed people to relieve the stress of daily facing such noxious realities. Those entering flooded houses donned masks to keep from inhaling spores from walls encrusted with multicolored mold. It was not too far fetched for a family to put face masks on members of the Holy Family in a front yard Nativity scene to symbolically protect the most important family of the season. While this act could be viewed as being just a touch of holiday humor, it is not too isolated from those ancient traditions of scaring off demons on Christmas Eve by beating drums and setting fires.

The addition of masks to this Nativity display reflects what many local residents had to wear as they cleared out their mold-infested homes. Photographer David Rae Morris took this photograph at a home in the Algiers neighborhood. (Courtesy of David Rae Morris)

Bingle had but similar to older photos I've seen that makes him look fluffier.

The hat and wings were my biggest concern. I replaced the felt on the wings. They were both made from celastic. [This is highly flammable and not easily available. It was used to create costumes and props such as armor and rocks.] I used acetone to re-soften the tip of the hat so it could be straightened. I fashioned a cone from an aluminum coke can and inserted it in the hat to straighten it. Light-weight spackle was used to re-form the tip of the hat. The cone was re-sanded and painted and clear crystals were glued to resemble sugar.

The eyes, nose, and the bell on Bingle's belly were carefully sanded and repainted. The girdle joining the upper part of Bingle to the lower part had to be replaced and refitted. An old leather belt that allows the legs to swing from the lower part of Bingle was cleaned and left as it was. It acts as a hinge. I added a new bow and a freshly painted candy cane.

Q: Was that the first time you have restored him?

A: Through the years Bingle has had some modifications. I remember three Bingle heads hanging in the shop. One had eyes made of light bulbs with the wires dangling from the head. I've seen pictures of this head used from the early days. The bunny suit was changed each year that I was there. In 1984, Oscar gave me the task of taking Bingle apart and fitting him with a new suit, hat, and wings. That experience helped me with restoring Bingle after

The Mr. Bingle marionette after its meticulous restoration. (Courtesy of Jeff Kent)

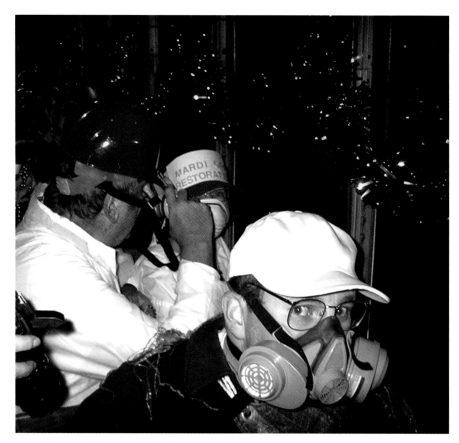

For their post-Katrina Twelfth Night streetcar ride, members of the Phunny Phorty Phellows Carnival krewe donned anti-mold protective masks as part of their costumes. (Photo by Jules Richard IV)

Katrina. So yes, Bingle was always going through facelifts through the years. I was told by Oscar the body was from an existing puppet when he created Bingle. That was pretty common to take parts from several different puppets to make a new character. In the shop we had boxes full of parts that read, "ARMS," "FEET," etc. He was restrung with monofilament string.

Q: Where is Bingle these days?

A: Bingle is in a closet at my parents' house. In the future I will donate him to The Historic New Orleans Collection.

When I first brought the Katrina-damaged Bingle to my parents' house, my mom gasped. She took him to the front yard, hung him on a tree, and sprayed Odor-Ban on him and talked to him as people drove by staring: "It's okay, Mr. Bingle, we'll take care of you." I was embarrassed

At holiday parties it was not unheard of to see an array of MREs, those military-supplied meals provided to hurricane victims, served up alongside traditional holiday foods. There are still MREs saved as souvenirs, not so unlike those snowballs saved in freezers after a rare New Orleans snowfall.

Katrina humor continued into the next year and the Carnival season when some members of the New Orleans Carnival krewe Phunny Phorty Phellows donned anti-mold masks for their annual Twelfth Night streetcar romp. During Mardi Gras there was no shortage of costumes turning anger into humor with the lampooning of everything from MREs to the Corps of Engineers and FEMA alongside impersonations of the various government officials deemed responsible for shoddy levee/floodwall construction and delayed government response to a desperate, flooding city.

The Crescent City has been no stranger to danger and heartache interfering with its Christmas celebration, whether during those scary days leading up to the Battle of New Orleans or the aftermaths of floods and hurricanes such as Betsy and Katrina, but this is a resilient city tempered with a lighthearted sense of humor that has helped the population move on.

Many of the costumes during the 2006 Carnival season reflected a Katrina theme. Here Jolie Bonck portrays "MRE Antoinette." MREs (Meal-Ready-to-Eat) were provided to hurricane victims by the military shortly after the storm. As queen of the Phunny Phorty Phellows, MRE Antoinette is shown boarding the St. Charles streetcar for the group's annual Twelfth Night ride. (Photo by Cheryl Gerber)

and asked her to do that in the backyard. When Bob Breck and others saw Bingle restored, they each bent down and talked to him. I don't talk to him, he's just a puppet! Maybe I really am crazy!

Years ago I realized the impact that Bingle had on people. He always brought smiles to those who watched him on TV or saw his window shows. It seems to make them giddy and they talk to him as if he is a small child or a cute puppy. I think when we see Bingle it brings back the childhood memories of Christmas when it was magical and really exciting. He makes us smile.

Through the years, I had taken Bingle to Children's Hospital and to an annual Christmas party for special kids, held by the New Orleans Fire Department's union. I took Bingle to Children's Hospital one year on Christmas Day to visit kids that were too ill to go home. As we walked into a room a young girl was in bed crying in pain. I began to feel I should not have walked in, but we were there and I gave it my best. When Bingle started flying around the room and "ice skating" on the floor, the tears stopped. Magic?

This Italian-made figure of the Christ child, damaged by Hurricane Katrina, is a reminder of survival and hope. (Photo by Peggy Scott Laborde)

Christmas Trees and the Hurricane

One of the casualties of Katrina during that first post-storm holiday season was the Christmas tree, which while available throughout the area, was in limited supply. One company that prior to the hurricane sold an average of four thousand trees during the Christmas season chose to skip the 2005 season altogether. After the storm, the lack of laborers, who were necessary to load and flock trees, forced the decision. There was also uncertainty concerning how many people in the area would buy trees and whether there were even enough houses that had survived the storm to make the sale of trees profitable. One dealer complained that he could not flock his trees because the warehouse where he had done the flocking had been blown down in the storm. Exacerbating these problems were the national shipping costs, which were much higher than normal.

In spite of the limiting circumstances, the big-box retailers reported that they had trees, and other independent dealers stocked them. Fears aside, people were willing to buy, and one dealer reported selling 20 percent of his entire stock in one day. Fourteen thousand trees that belonged to a tree farmer in Pearl River, Louisiana, were blown over during the storm, but with help he had been able to right the trees and expected to have one of his best years ever due to a lack of competition from other tree growers.

Evergreen Agricultural Enterprises gave away five hundred trees as part of the city's official tree lighting ceremony downtown on Canal Street. Many of the street's towering newly planted palm trees had been toppled by Katrina's howling winds. The fronds of the fallen palms pointed to the south, toward the Mississippi River, showing how the storm's winds tore across the city from the north. By Christmas 2006 the palm trees were once again upright and had greatly multiplied in number. Beginning that Christmas season, their trunks were covered with tiny jewel-like lights. Wreaths were hung on Canal's cast-iron light standards along with red bows and garlands. In 2007 the sight was more lavish, and even more so in 2008 as Canal Street once again took on a brilliant display of electric lights reminiscent of the city's holidays in the late nineteenth century.

After the holidays, many of the area's Christmas trees are used in different ways. While some remain standing in local homes, decked out in purple, green, and gold beads as "Mardi Gras trees," since the early 1990s more and more Christmas trees have been collected and deposited into Louisiana's marshes to help rebuild the wetlands. These coastal wetlands are New Orleans' first line of defense from hurricanes. The idea came from the Netherlands, where willow trees and other shrubs are tied together to help create thousands of acres of stable land along that country's north coast. The use of discarded Christmas trees was suggested as a good substitute, especially since the sap prevents them from breaking down quickly. Known as sediment fencing, the trees are placed in a series of wooden frameworks called "cribs" that trap sediment, allowing plants to take root and strengthen the marshes.

Trees have been placed in such spots as Goose Bayou in the lower part of Jefferson Parish, while in Orleans Parish, after the Christmas of 2007, trees were deposited in Bayou Sauvage, located in the hurricane-vulnerable eastern part of the city. After all, the trees are readily available every January and rather than sending them to the landfill they might just help prevent another Katrina-like storm surge from inundating New Orleans and washing away future Christmases.

For the first Christmas after Hurricane Katrina, the InterContinental Hotel erected in its lobby an enormous tree topped by a fleur-de-lis. (Photo by Peggy Scott Laborde)

A second-line parade opens festivities for the annual menorah-lighting ceremony held at the Riverwalk Marketplace. (Photo by David Rae Morris)

CHAPTER ELEVEN
Hanukkah

An ever-increasing aspect of the modern holiday season in New Orleans is the celebration of the ancient Jewish holiday of Hanukkah. Hanukkah commemorates the time more than two thousand years ago when the Maccabees, the rebel army of Judah Maccabee, defeated the dictatorial grip of the Greek-Assyrian ruler Antiochus IV. The victorious Jews reclaimed the temple on Jerusalem's Mount Moriah, cleansing and rededicating the house of worship. It was said that they could find only one day's supply of purified oil to be used for illuminating the temple, but miraculously the oil lasted the eight days necessary to replenish the supply. Thus the eight days of Hanukkah, with the corresponding eight candles of the menorah, is a celebration of freedom.

Historically, Hanukkah is a relatively minor holiday in the Jewish calendar. In recent years its proximity to Christmas at the end of the western calendar year has brought it greater attention. Hanukkah begins on the twenty-fifth day of the Hebrew month of Kislev and like Mardi Gras is a floating holiday, so it does not always coincide with Christmas.

Called the Festival of Light, it is especially appealing because of its child-centered aspect, the presentation of gifts, and the consumption of traditional dishes. Many Hanukkah foods are cooked in oil to commemorate the oil in the temple. The twinkling firelight of the menorah fits well into the same realm of winter festival to which Christmas has long been linked.

Customarily, Jews have chosen either to avoid Christmas altogether, a near impossibility, or to embrace at least the secular side of the event by putting up trees and exchanging gifts with family members. In New Orleans it is not unusual for Reform Jewish families to light a menorah and put up a Christmas tree.

Although many New Orleans-area Jews do take part in the city's Christmas festivities, celebrations commemorating the Jewish holiday abound. Chabad-Lubavitch of Louisiana, a Hasidic Jewish organization that provides educational, social, and religious programs for the entire Jewish community, has presented the lighting of the largest menorah in Louisiana since 1989. Hanukkah at the Riverwalk is hosted by the Riverwalk Marketplace at the foot of Canal Street, along the Mississippi River, in downtown New Orleans. Along with

Rabbi Mendel Rivkin, left, presides at the annual menorah-lighting ceremony held at the Riverwalk Marketplace during Hanukkah. During the 2007 ceremony, and in honor of Israel's sixtieth anniversary, members of the local Jewish community who had served in the Israeli Defense Forces were invited to be part of a "living menorah." The annual event is organized by Chabad-Lubavitch of Louisiana. (Photo by Brad Edelman)

the lighting of a menorah, to celebrate the message of religious freedom and tolerance, there is contemporary Jewish music and free traditional foods such as latkes, potato pancakes fried in the all-important oil. A few miles away at 6227 St. Charles Avenue, Temple Sinai celebrates Hanukkah on the Avenue with its own ceremonial public menorah lighting. Also participating is the temple's youth choir.

Touro Infirmary archivist Catherine "Cathy" Kahn is a descendent of the Danziger family, owners of Danziger's, one of nineteenth-century New Orleans' premier dry goods stores. According to Kahn, this emporium was noted for its day-after-Christmas sales. She describes the Danzigers as a Jewish family that was both "assimilated and eccentric."

The family always had a menorah during the Hanukkah celebration and depending upon the holiday's proximity to Christmas, the menorah's candles might have even been lit in the "twinkling lights of the Christmas tree." The family said prayers over the lighting of each candle and sang "Rock of Ages"—not the Christian hymn, but a Jewish one of the same name with a different tune and words. "Rock of Ages" is a song of victory over the enemy: "When Thy word broke their sword with Thy saving power."

New Orleans councilmember-at-large Arnie Fielkow lights the menorah at Chabad-Lubavitch of Louisiana's annual menorah-lighting ceremony held at the Riverwalk Marketplace. (Photo by Brad Edelman)

The Danzigers were members of the Reform congregation of Temple Sinai, which was founded in 1870. Kahn recalls, "If you wandered into Temple Sinai before World War II and heard a service, it was all in English except for the Kaddish and Shema [creed]. This was all I ever knew in Hebrew until after World War II. Hymns were words given to Beethoven and Brahms and always in English."

The family was from Alsace-Lorraine in France, and, says Kahn, "If your family came from France to New Orleans, even if Jewish, you are more of the fabric of the Creoles, even more so than the 'Kaintucks' who came here from up the river." She feels that "keeping kosher in New Orleans means never eating raw oysters in a month without an *r*," a reference to the popular belief that, prior to refrigeration, months that contained the letter *r* were periods when oysters were at their peak of freshness.

Following the lighting of the menorah and the singing of "Rock of Ages," the family sang traditional Christmas carols such as "O Holy Night" and "O Little Town of Bethlehem." Hers was a musical family and they always sang in the evenings with her mother playing the piano and her father on the clarinet or one of several other instruments he played. Their songs ranged from hymns and Christmas carols to the music of Gilbert and Sullivan, which remains among Cathy's favorites.

The young audience is clearly engaged at the menorah-lighting ceremony held at the Riverwalk Marketplace. (Photo courtesy of David Kaufmann)

From her memories as a young person growing up in a family that adhered to classic Reform Judaism, Kahn recalls that every Jewish family she knew in New Orleans had a Christmas tree. Her own family's tree extended from floor to ceiling. They had a tree every year except when her father served as president of Temple Sinai between 1943 and 1946; while serving in that position, he felt that a Christmas tree might be inappropriate. When his term in office ended, a tree went up again the following December. Christmas presents were exchanged, although the family had never heard of Hanukkah presents at the time. They ate Christmas dinner, which was in the traditional New Orleans style with turkey, oyster dressing, and *bûche de Noël,* the French Christmas log cake. At the time Kahn had never eaten what is now considered traditional Hanukkah fare such as latkes.

As her children grew older and married spouses from other parts of the country where there were more Orthodox Jewish families, Kahn came to recognize the differences between the more relaxed celebration of Hanukkah in New Orleans and the ways it was celebrated in other areas. "I have to say it's always a revelation. We didn't realize there was a difference."

A prospective daughter-in-law from Long Island, New York, came to visit during the holidays one year and the young woman "freaked" when she saw the family's Christmas tree. To compensate, Kahn brought in a potted plant, not unlike Christmas trees in 1850s New Orleans. She placed it on the other side of the room and decorated it with naked Ken and Barbie dolls to serve as Adam and Eve and added a rubber snake and an apple. She presented it as an "Old Testament tree," causing the young lady to laugh so hard at the gesture that everything then got off on the right footing.

After this event, Christmas trees were phased out of the Kahn house in order to provide the grandchildren with an understanding of their own Jewish heritage. At the same time many other New Orleans Jewish families were doing the same sort of thing, as the local celebration of Hanukkah began to follow more mainstream American Judaism.

Kahn regards her earlier New Orleans celebration as an "Episcopal 'wannabe' version" of the holidays. Now to get her Episcopal holiday "fix" she visits New Iberia and celebrates with a daughter and Episcopal son-in-law who put up an old-fashioned Christmas tree. On Christmas Eve they light all of the candles on the menorah at once and sing Jewish hymns, allowing the children to experience the real meaning of Hanukkah and the freedom that this ancient holiday represents.

The poinsettia exhibit in City Park's Conservatory of the Two Sisters is one of many botanical exhibits on display during Celebration in the Oaks. (Photo by Coleen Perilloux Landry)

CHAPTER 12

Christmas Present

Celebration in the Oaks

A whistle cuts through the winter night and suddenly there's the train, all lit up and filled with passengers returning from their journey through ancient oaks adorned with tiny white lights shaped like doves. At Christmastime almost two million lights illuminate one of America's largest urban parks.

What began in the mid-1980s as a tiny Christmas celebration of decorated trees and a few choral performances has blossomed into a major attraction featuring nightly entertainment by local school choirs and dance groups. City Park is aglow from late November through early January with its Celebration in the Oaks.

Highlights include a restored century-old carousel and amusement rides. Also on view is the New Orleans Historic Train Garden, a

During City Park's Celebration in the Oaks, decorated trees and lighting enhance one of New Orleans' most beloved green spaces. (Photo by Coleen Perilloux Landry)

195

In 2005 the Mr. Bingle that once hung above the front entrance to Maison Blanche on Canal Street found a new home at City Park's Celebration in the Oaks. (Photo by Coleen Perilloux Landry)

The restored antique carousel is a highlight of City Park's Carousel Gardens Amusement Park, especially during Celebration in the Oaks. The carousel features a menagerie of fifty-four hand-carved animals and is listed on the National Register of Historic Places. (Photo by Coleen Perilloux Landry)

Storyland provides entertainment for children all year, but it is especially magical during Celebration in the Oaks. (Photo by Coleen Perilloux Landry)

fourteen-thousand-square-foot elevated display through which model trains and streetcars run on fourteen hundred feet of track. The display showcases over forty of New Orleans' landmark buildings, all in miniature but big-time impressive.

Open at night during the season is Storyland. Featuring twenty-six exhibits that engage the imagination, young visitors can come face to face with their favorite storybook characters and climb on, slide down, or crawl through the fairy-tale attractions.

Nearby is the Conservatory of the Two Sisters. Beneath its imposing glass dome is a poinsettia exhibit, with an oversized poinsettia "tree."

Reenactments of the Nativity are also presented. For many years some of the figures from the Nativity that once stood in the yard of the decorated Centanni home on Canal Street were used. To help City Park start its lighting display, Popeyes Chicken and Biscuits founder Al Copeland, who decorated his own home at Christmastime for over thirty years, followed the example of the Centannis and donated some lighted figures to the park, including a giant Santa.

One of the more modern features, located in the Botanical Garden, is a laser screen thirty feet wide and twenty feet high. It lights up according to the tempo of the music played. The nine- to eleven-minute-long animated laser shows include images that correspond to the lyrics of Christmas songs recorded by New Orleans musicians.

In 2005 the Mr. Bingle sculpture that hung for so many years in front of Maison Blanche on Canal Street and later in front of Dillard's Lakeside found a new home at Celebration in the Oaks. After a successful fundraising drive to pay for the restoration of

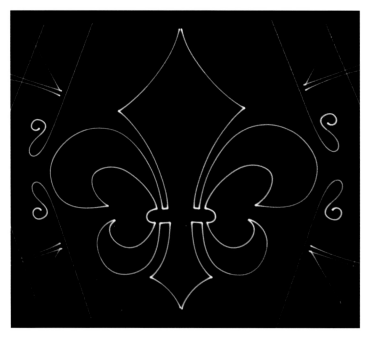

Visitors to Celebration in the Oaks are treated to a laser show that includes the animation of Christmas songs recorded by New Orleans musicians. Laser Spectacles, Inc. created the screen and tailored the technology especially for City Park. (Courtesy of Laser Spectacles, Inc.)

Santa floats atop a French Quarter balcony during a laser show at Celebration in the Oaks. (Courtesy of Laser Spectacles, Inc.)

the giant-sized version of the tiny snowman, Mr. Bingle is now a permanent part of the Celebration exhibit.

Other area lighting displays include Celebration of the Season at Lafreniere Park in Metairie, to which the lighted figures that once adorned the home of the late Al Copeland have been donated. During December the City of Kenner has a Magical Christmas Village Celebration. Located in Rivertown at Veterans Century of Sentries Park next to City Hall, the display features small decorated cottages, lights, and live musical entertainment. Taking place the first two weekends in December is the Holiday of Lights at the Tammany Trace Trailhead in Mandeville, on the Northshore.

Downtown Decorations

For many years the Downtown Development District (DDD), a business improvement district that focuses on the downtown area, has sponsored a music-filled Canal Street tree-lighting ceremony. The mayor of New Orleans does the honors in pressing the ceremonial switch

Several downtown hotels have joined in the decorating for the holidays in a big way. The Ritz-Carlton features a life-sized cottage made of chocolate and candy and a gargantuan decorated tree in the courtyard. The hotel presents tea parties with Papa Noël on weekends throughout the season.

The Sheraton erects a giant Cajun Santa, complete with alligators instead of reindeer in its lobby. Santa can be seen by passersby through the enormous window fronting Canal Street.

The InterContinental New Orleans has gotten into the Christmas spirit with a large decorated tree at the foot of a lobby stairway and a cottage made of gingerbread. During the holidays the hotel features a Gingerbread Tea that includes music, cookie decorating, visits from elves, and as the hotel puts it, an appearance by "the Big Man Himself."

Windsor Court also decorates a tree in their lobby and Harrah's Hotel installs a miniature replica in gingerbread of a local landmark in its lobby each year.

The historic City Park Peristyle is beautifully illuminated during Celebration in the Oaks. (Photo by Alex Demyan)

The Popp Bandstand is yet another setting for illumination during City Park's annual Celebration in the Oaks. (Photo by Alex Demyan)

An angel is one of the symbols of City Park's Celebration in the Oaks. (Photo by Alex Demyan)

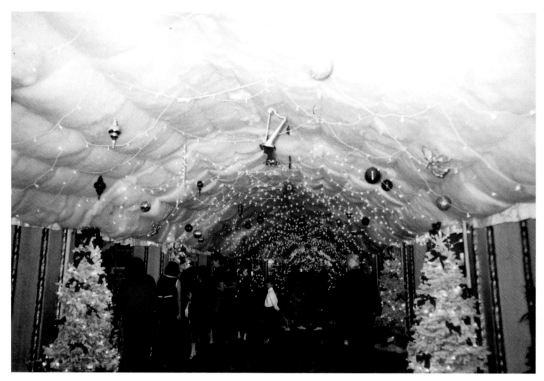

The lobby of the Roosevelt Hotel, formerly the Fairmont, has long been decorated for the holidays. Its "snowy" canopy transports visitors to a winter wonderland. (Photo by Peggy Scott Laborde)

Emily Danove Degan stands in front of the life-size gingerbread cottage in the lobby of the Fairmont Hotel, now known by its former name, the Roosevelt. (Photo by Peggy Scott Laborde)

During the Christmas season the Sheraton on downtown Canal Street erects a Cajun Christmas display complete with Santa and a sleigh pulled by alligators. (Courtesy Sheraton New Orleans Hotel)

The ultimate destination for enjoying downtown decorations is the lobby of the grand old hotel that was originally called the Grunewald, then Roosevelt, Fairmont, and with a $100 million renovation completed in 2009 reopened with the return of the Roosevelt name. New ownership continues to transform the block-long lobby into a winter wonderland with flocked trees, a canopy of "snow," and ornaments hanging from the ceiling.

Miracle on Fulton Street, presented by Harrah's Casino, is an almost half-block-long canopy of white fleur-de-lis ornaments and thousands of lights. The display is lined with twelve-foot-tall Christmas trees. A special feature is a periodic "snowfall."

Holiday Home Tour

Ever wished you could get a peek beyond the gates of New Orleans Garden District mansions? That wish can easily be fulfilled by taking the Preservation Resource Center of New Orleans' annual Holiday Home Tour.

In early December, you can visit seven lavishly decorated homes in this self-guided walking tour that covers a section of one of the city's most historic neighborhoods. Small music groups perform at

Formerly the Maison Blanche department store, the Ritz-Carlton on historic Canal Street celebrates the season with such lavish decorations as a life-size gingerbread house. The gingerbread house is a scaled replica of a Garden District mansion. It takes two months of preparation work and five days to assemble. Four engineers and six pastry chefs complete the task. Among its myriad ingredients, the structure contains 800 pounds of icing, 432 pounds of flour, 179 pounds of refined sugar, and 108 pounds of brown sugar. Add to all this 200 pounds of candy! (Photo by Peggy Scott Laborde)

each home during the tour. Since you may be in the shopping mode at that point, check out the Home Tour boutique, often featuring locally themed merchandise. Tour proceeds help promote the preservation and restoration of New Orleans' historic architecture and neighborhoods.

Caroling in Washington Square

Lesser known than Jackson or Lafayette Squares, but still delightful, is Washington Square in the heart of the Marigny neighborhood. In early December the Faubourg Marigny Improvement Association holds this intimate evening of caroling that is a scaled-down version of the Jackson Square caroling later in the season. (See Chapter Four.) Children from the nearby Girls and Boys Town center light the decorated tree. Earlier that day an arts market is held in the square.

A decorated tree with giant blue ornaments stands in the atrium of the Ritz-Carlton hotel. (Courtesy of The Ritz-Carlton, New Orleans)

Presented by Harrah's Casino, Miracle on Fulton Street attracts visitors to a canopy of lights and fleur-de-lis ornaments that spans Fulton Street at Poydras Street in downtown New Orleans. There's even a "snowfall" at regular intervals. (Photo by Peggy Scott Laborde)

Long Vue House and Gardens

Located at 7 Bamboo Road, just east of the Jefferson Parish line, the home of late philanthropists and art collectors Mr. and Mrs. Edgar Stern is open to the public and decorated with local greenery for the holidays. A highlight during the season is Long Vue's holiday teas.

Ornaments That Do Good

Since 1993, New Orleans-based artist and designer Mignon Faget has designed ornaments that she calls "AdornAments," celebrating the historic preservation of New Orleans architecture. The first in the series of wearable Christmas ornaments celebrated the Gallier House, the historic 1850s French Quarter home of architect James Gallier, Jr.

In 1996, Faget began designing an annual holiday AdornAment to benefit the Preservation Resource Center (PRC) of New Orleans and the many programs it supports. Each year a percentage of sales are donated to the PRC.

Since the early 1990s, jewelry designer Mignon Faget has designed what she calls holiday "AdornAments" celebrating the historic preservation of New Orleans architecture. Since 1996, a percentage of AdornAment sales has been donated to the Preservation Resource Center. This AdornAment depicts the historic Doullut Steamboat House, located in the Holy Cross neighborhood. (Courtesy of Mignon Faget)

Festivus

One of the more offbeat holiday markets of the many that pop up around Christmas is called Festivus. Staged at the Crescent City Farmers' Market on the first three Sundays of December, it features locally made arts and crafts and borrows its name from a *Seinfeld* episode. Look for gifts made from recycled objects. A highlight is the "re-gifting station," where patrons bring something they can definitely part with and exchange it for something they would hopefully enjoy more.

According to Crescent City Farmers' Market director Richard McCarthy, the concept was inspired by the *Seinfeld* character of Frank Costanza. Worn down by years of competitive holiday shopping with his son George, he decided to create his own holiday.

Suburban Shopping

Today most malls in the New Orleans area offer youngsters the chance to meet and take photos with Santa while their parents finish up the seasonal shopping. Along with Santa, Lakeside Shopping Center features an impressive Christmas village that includes a miniature train display. Over the last few years the mall has promoted

Santa awaits a visit from the next child in line at Clearview Mall in suburban Metairie. (Photo by Peggy Scott Laborde)

Even the historic New Orleans streetcar is decorated during the Christmas season. (Photo by Peggy Scott Laborde)

Long a part of the New Orleans skyline is the tower of what was the Hibernia Bank building (now Capital One). The tower is colorfully illuminated during many holidays. (Photo by Alex Demyan)

a Santa's Snowfall nightly, with a faux flurry. Dillard's is one of the anchor stores in the mall and sells Mr. Bingle memorabilia. That little snowman with the ice-cream-cone hat has become one of the symbols of New Orleans Christmas.

The Nutcracker *and Messiah*

New Orleans-area productions of Tchaikovsky's *The Nutcracker* abound during the Christmas season. The longest annual presentation is the one mounted by the Delta Festival Ballet with music provided by the Louisiana Philharmonic Orchestra. Among other area productions, two are staged by the New Orleans Ballet Theatre and the Jefferson Ballet Theatre.

"Alleluia" is certainly in the air at Christmas, and the Louisiana Philharmonic Orchestra's presentation of Handel's Messiah, in conjunction with the Symphony Chorus of New Orleans, is a local holiday staple.

Holiday on the Boulevard and Kwanzaa

Holiday on the Boulevard is a series of events that takes place along Oretha Castle Haley Boulevard. Local bands, storytelling, food, crafts, and characters from the past are featured in this weekend-long event in December. It is coordinated by the Ashé Cultural Arts Center.

Ashé is also home to an annual Kwanzaa celebration. This weeklong festival (December 26-January 1) honors African-American heritage. Consisting of candle lighting and gift giving and culminating in a feast, it was created by black political activist and author Ron Karenga and first celebrated in California in 1967.

Happy New Year!

What makes New Orleans' public celebration of New Year's Eve a bit unique is the giant display of fireworks that lights up the midnight sky over the Mississippi River. The pyrotechnics are actually set off from a barge in the middle of the river, with the French Quarter on one side and the quaint historic community of Algiers Point on the other, but of course the streaks across the sky can be seen from miles away.

In the Quarter itself, a giant papier-mâché gumbo pot on top of the Jax Brewery shopping complex, located on the Mississippi River, was dropped for many years. In 2008 the pot was replaced by a black and gold lighted fleur-de-lis, nine feet high by six feet wide, which sits atop a twenty-five-foot-high pole. On the sixth-floor terrace of the former brewery is an equally giant papier-mâché New Year's baby. There's also a stage near Jackson Square featuring local bands before the big event. The music, fireworks, and drop are coordinated by a

Fireworks at midnight over the Mississippi River are a New Orleans New Year's Eve tradition. (Photo by Alex Demyan)

group called the Crescent City Countdown Club in cooperation with the City of New Orleans and the New Orleans Tourism and Marketing Corporation. The steamboat *Natchez* has a New Year's Eve dinner dance cruise that affords a front-seat view of the fireworks.

The French Quarter is not the only place to celebrate on New Year's Eve. In New Orleans' Mid-City neighborhood, across from John Dibert Elementary School on the Orleans Avenue neutral ground, a bonfire has grown into a citywide event. Although most locals associate bonfires with Christmas Eve and upriver parishes, some neighborhood residents estimate that the Mid-City ritual began as long ago as seventy-five years.

What started as a neighborhood's family-oriented get-together to dispose of Christmas trees has gradually turned into an enormous, sometimes wild street party. By 2008, there were safety concerns, especially when some attendees added fireworks to the giant blaze and shot off bottle rockets into the crowd. No longer can revelers circle the fire only inches away from the flames. There are now barricades and strict monitoring by the police and fire departments, but in the spirit of the season, the show has gone on.

In 2008 a fleur-de-lis replaced the gumbo pot atop Jax Brewery as the city's focus during the New Year's countdown. (Photo by Syndey Byrd)

In Mid-City a New Year's Eve bonfire takes place on the Orleans Avenue neutral ground. Ian McNulty, Mid-City resident and author of A Season of Night: New Orleans Life after Katrina, *describes the setting: "There is this blazing pyre so hot it's searing your face, there are little rockets shrieking helter skelter and popping into spark blossoms above the oak trees, and there are people drinking, banging on drums or tossing little handwritten messages about the year's regrets into the oblivion of the fire. And people tow their kids around in little wagons, or set up blankets on the neutral ground to watch the whole thing like some surreal nighttime picnic. It's chaotic, exhilarating and somehow family-oriented all at once. Which is something that makes a lot of sense in New Orleans, especially when you know the start of Carnival season is just days away." (Photo by Ian McNulty)*

A New Year's Eve bonfire fan wears her good wishes for the New Year. (Photo by Ian McNulty)

The Sugar Bowl

By the 1920s the New Year was considered the official end of the Christmas holidays, and in 1935 a new tradition was born in New Orleans. The *New Orleans States* said, "The great Sugar Bowl classic which has been on the lips of the football fans here for almost a year becomes a reality today."

That year New Year's Eve was more boisterous than it had been in some time. The *New Orleans States* said it was "featured by the noisiest and most enthusiastic greeting to a new year since the depression. New Orleans today was observing the holiday with the Sugar Bowl."

"Great Inaugural Sugar Bowl Grid Tilt in Prospect," headlined the *Times-Picayune* on the first day of '35. "T.N.T. Tulane 'n' Temple!" heralded the newspaper. From miles around people were expected to stream into the city, and the *Picayune* surmised that unless "all the signs fail and the experts miss their guesses" there would be a capacity crowd at Tulane Stadium. Unsettled weather brought fears that the game would be dampened by rain, but while there were clouds, not a drop of rain fell on the game. The bowl was declared a success—even more so since the hometown team of Tulane University defeated Philadelphia's Temple University by a score of 20 to 14.

Many years in the making, the Sugar Bowl game was the brainchild of *Item* sports editor Fred Digby and that paper's publisher, James M. Thomson. Their campaign, which began in 1927, called for a mid-winter group of amateur sports events highlighted by a major college football game. The Rose Bowl in Pasadena, California, started in 1902 and along with that city's Rose Parade, successfully drew national attention and tourists to the area. Digby and his boss at the *Item* felt that a similar event would do the same for New Orleans. By the early 1930s, with the Great Depression embracing the nation, such a mid-winter extravaganza was more than ever seen as a much-needed way to boost the local economy during a traditionally slow time in tourism.

Warren V. Miller and Joseph M. Cousins, among others, took up the gauntlet and helped create the New Orleans Mid-Winter Sports Association in 1934. A guarantee of financing was quickly secured, and the first Sugar Bowl game was slated for January 1, 1935. The trophy was a large silver bowl made in London in 1830 and donated to the association by the Royal Street antique dealer Waldhorn's.

The *States* saw the event as a permanent fixture capable of attracting thousands of visitors every year, and in 1935 the newspaper reported, "The hotels are crowded with football fans who have come in from all parts." Among the visitors were two hundred people from Temple, and overall fifteen states were represented in the stands. The *Item* reported that "the Sugar Bowl . . . will be attended by scores of fashionables. . . . Numbers of cocktail parties are being given before and after the game." Furthermore, the *Item* commended the "concentration on New Orleans of the whole country's football public" and concluded that as a result "New Orleans itself wins in every way."

Within a year of the first game plans were afoot to enlarge Tulane

One of New Orleans' most noted twentieth-century political cartoonists was John
Chase, who drew the covers of several early Sugar Bowl programs such as this one for
the 1940 Notre Dame versus Alabama game. (Gift of the Sugar Bowl; The Historic
New Orleans Collection)

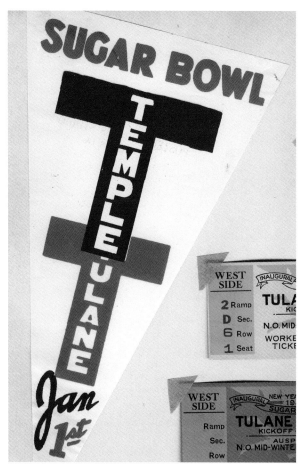

The first Sugar Bowl, in which Tulane defeated Temple, was played in 1935, forever changing New Year's in New Orleans. (Gift of the Sugar Bowl; The Historic New Orleans Collection)

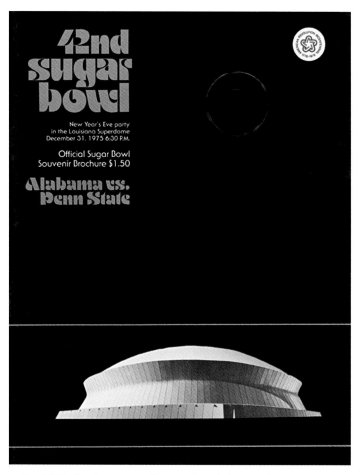

In 1975 the Sugar Bowl was played for the first time in the newly built Louisiana Superdome. Cold weather would never again be a hindrance during the winter game. (Gift of the Sugar Bowl; The Historic New Orleans Collection)

Stadium in anticipation of growing attendance. This proved to be a wise move, since in 1937 a crowd of 42,000, then the largest crowd ever in attendance at a New Orleans sports event, witnessed California's Santa Clara University defeat Louisiana State University. Eliza Ripley may have complained in 1912 that New Year's Day had become rather tame and quiet, but a quarter of a century later the *Times-Picayune* was able to say "more than any other thing, the Sugar Bowl game changed holiday quiet to holiday excitement in New Orleans."

In 1939 the Mid-Winter Sports Association sponsored a bond drive and in just over a month raised $550,000 to finance the enlargement of Tulane Stadium to a seating capacity of 69,000. Further additions eventually brought its capacity to almost 81,000, at that time one of the largest stadiums in the country.

The prestige of the Sugar Bowl was growing. In 1939 and 1940, Texas Christian and Texas A&M were respective winners at the Sugar Bowl, and both teams were voted national champions by the poll of the Associated Press. The Sugar Bowl chose not to cancel during World War II, and although attendance was down, by the end of the

Photographer Dorothy Violet Gulledge snapped this nighttime shot on Canal Street in the 1950s. Note the neon sign welcoming Sugar Bowl visitors. (Louisiana Division/City Archives, New Orleans Public Library)

war it rebounded, reaching 75,000 in 1946.

During the late 1950s and early 1960s the Sugar Bowl was dogged by civil rights issues over permitting black players from states with racially integrated teams to play. Louisiana's discriminatory segregation laws forced the Sugar Bowl to lose prestige and slip into becoming merely a Southern regional event. With the Civil Rights Act of 1964, the Sugar Bowl emerged once again as a major player in the bowl circuit and with each New Year vied with the Rose Bowl, Orange Bowl, and Cotton Bowl, which began in 1937, for recognition, attendance, and television time. An exciting moment for the Sugar Bowl was New Year's Eve, 1975, the year Alabama beat Penn State. After forty-one games at Tulane Stadium the bowl game was played for the first time in the new Louisiana Superdome.

The importance of the Sugar Bowl in the national college football arena was enhanced when it was named one of the rotating bowls of the BCS (Bowl Championship Series) for the national championship title game. The trophy for the winner of this game is a large Waterford crystal football.

The Mid-Winter Sports Association calendar has always included more than football, although the Sugar Bowl game garners the most attention. There have been outdoor track and field events, tennis tournaments, basketball games, boxing matches, a golf tournament, and yacht races on Lake Pontchartrain. In the twenty-first century, competition has come to include volleyball, soccer, lacrosse, and track and field. Even though under the Sugar Bowl banner, some of these events have also been held at other times of the year.

The Rose Bowl is the oldest bowl game, but New Orleans shares "second oldest" honors with Miami's Orange Bowl, which also played its first game on New Year's, 1935. In both cities the big games helped promote their relatively mild winter destinations.

Since its inception, the Sugar Bowl football game has symbolized the New Year in New Orleans. The game has traditionally been held on the afternoon of January 1, but in the more recent past it has been moved to other dates to cooperate with the television schedules of other bowl games and enhance its standings in the national arena of college football.

The New Orleans Bowl

In 2001, the New Orleans Bowl was launched. This is a post-season National Collegiate Athletic Association (NCAA) certified game that pits a team from Conference USA against the champions of the Sun Belt Conference. It is held around Christmas, often the Sunday before Christmas, and is played at the Louisiana Superdome.

CHAPTER THIRTEEN

The End of Christmas, the Start of Carnival

Softening the blow of any post-festivity letdown at the close of the Christmas holidays in New Orleans is the arrival of the Carnival season. No longer is Twelfth Night in the Crescent City merely the end of the religious Christmas observance; instead, it marks the beginning of the expanding period that culminates in Mardi Gras.

Epiphany

Twelfth Night, the last evening of the Twelve Days of Christmas, began as a religious ritual to mark Epiphany on January 6, commemorating the Magi's visit to the Christ child. At the Council of Tours in 567 the twelve days between Christmas and Epiphany were proclaimed to be a single sacred and festive season.

These twelve religious days are counted differently from one country to another. In some the number includes Christmas Day, while in others the countdown begins the day after Christmas. In England, Twelfth Night falls on January 5, the Eve of the Epiphany, while January 6 is the twelfth day. New Orleans celebrates Twelfth Night on the night of January 6, the night of the twelfth day. No matter when the observation of Twelfth Night falls, it is the formal end of Christmas. By tradition in many places, all Christmas decorations should be taken down after Twelfth Night.

The term "epiphany" is derived from the Greek word *epiphania*, or manifestation, and can represent various revelations of the glory and divinity of Christ as celebrated by Christians. The celebration of Epiphany probably originated in the Eastern Orthodox Church (Constantinople) and marked any of several incidences of this manifestation of Christ: Christ's baptism, when a dove descended overhead and proclaimed him the son of God; the Miracle at Cana, when water was changed to wine; the Feeding of the Multitudes; and most importantly today, the visit of the Magi and their recognition of Christ with their presentation of gifts. By the second century, January 6 was celebrated by some adherents of the eastern church as the actual birth of Christ. In the fourth century, Rome adopted December 25 as the official birth date, and despite some resistance in the east, the focus of the Epiphany shifted to the Nativity and the visit of the Magi.

Twelfth Night

Especially true during the Middle Ages and Renaissance, Twelfth Night ultimately became a time of giving lavish gifts. It began as a religious observance but evolved into a high-spirited festive time marked by parties, balls, and banquets.

The center of the parties was the Twelfth Night cake, a confection that dates back to about the thirteenth century. A bean or some other token was hidden inside the cake and whoever received the piece with the bean became the monarch of the party. In France such cakes were called *gateau des rois,* or kings' cake; this pastry, also called "king cake" is a treasured part of the New Orleans celebration not just on Twelfth Night but throughout the entire Carnival season.

While in modern New Orleans the recipient of the bean, now almost always a plastic baby, is supposed to host the next party, in the Middle Ages the winner of the bean became the Lord of Misrule, ruling a world turned boisterously upside down. The mock king supervised an evening that was generally rowdy with dancing, singing, gaming, eating, and drinking. A great deal of noise and laughter prevailed during this merry and often irreligious celebration. There was also masking and the exchange of roles, whereby the master bowed down to the servant and men and women often cross-dressed.

Twelfth Night was a popular celebration in France, but across the English Channel it was notoriously riotous. In England it was once a great day of merry making, but by the mid-nineteenth century it had fallen from favor. The Twelfth Night cake evolved into the Christmas cake. English-born resident of New Orleans T. K. Wharton in his journals of the 1850s and early 1860s did not make mention of Twelfth Night, even though he made his fondness for all the activities surrounding Christmas and New Year's Day perfectly clear.

Twelfth Night celebrations had little hold in the United States with the nation's puritanical beginnings. In many parts of the country Twelfth Night, like Christmas with its feasting, drunkenness, and rowdiness, was unappealing to the rising middle class, and while those who celebrated Christmas might have considered Twelfth Night the end of Christmas, the holiday had mostly slipped from view.

This de-emphasis was exemplified in New Orleans, where after the American victory over the British at the Battle of New Orleans, January 8 replaced Twelfth Night as the local ending to the holiday season for about half a century. This way

The invitation to the first Carnival ball of the Twelfth Night Revelers in 1870, with its decorations of holly and ivy, shows how the Epiphany was still considered a part of the Christmas holiday in New Orleans and not necessarily the start of the Carnival season. (The Historic New Orleans Collection)

of thinking fit comfortably with the sober-minded patriotism that marked the first half of the nineteenth century across the country.

As the celebration of Christmas became more secular in the United States, for some the religious meaning of the Epiphany and Twelfth Night lost its importance. Decorations once had been put up on Christmas Eve and taken down on Epiphany. By the late nineteenth century, and especially in the twentieth, as the Christmas season developed a looser definition than the days between Christmas and Epiphany, decorations seemed to go up earlier and earlier in late November to be pulled down as early as the day after Christmas or New Year's Day. The giving of gifts on Twelfth Night fell out of practice. In New Orleans this was obvious by the tendency of Anglo-Americans such as T. K. Wharton to exchange presents on Christmas Eve or Christmas Day, while the city's Creoles exchanged small gifts on Christmas Day and the better ones on New Year's Day.

The Twelfth Night Revelers

In New Orleans it turns out that the celebration of Twelfth Night was not entirely forgotten; it had only gone underground for a few decades, to be revived in a different form. Creole New Orleans traditionally began its Carnival season on Twelfth Night with private balls and parties complete with a *gateau des rois* from which a king or queen who was expected to give the next gathering was chosen. It is from these first parties that the season's round of balls would grow.

The *New Orleans Times* in 1870 wrote, "The bean cake, much in vogue even now among certain of our Creole families" had been introduced about 1336 when Twelfth Night "became rather a social feast than a religious one." The *Times* lamented, "As time wore on, [Twelfth Night] gradually declined to a period for more private sociality."

On January 6, 1870, the celebration of Twelfth Night came to New Orleans in its most public manner to date with the inauguration of a parade and ball of a new organization calling itself the Twelfth Night Revelers. The *Times* applauded its founders, arguing that the ancient holiday of Twelfth Night "is surely worthy of honor from a Christian community; and thanks to the Twelfth Night Revelers, it was celebrated last evening, in a manner at least creditable to its antiquity." The newspaper took a jab at the Puritans by saying, "It is fit . . . that in a country where holidays have been almost totally abolished by the Puritanical element introduced in its early settlement that some of the most notable ones should be revived in consonant with the changing spirit of the age we live in, and among all no one is more beautifully appropriate than that of Twelfth Night."

The *Times* went still further to extol the economic and social benefits the new krewe could offer. With a viewpoint that sounds like something asserted by one of today's tourist officials, the *Times* continued, "None can deny but that holiday celebrations benefit every branch of business in the community, by throwing a large sum of money into active circulation, a considerable portion of which comes from abroad."

King cakes have become the culinary symbol of the New Orleans Carnival season. (Photo by Peggy Scott Laborde)

The *Daily Picayune* was equally enthused by the Twelfth Night Revelers, proclaiming, "The carnival season was inaugurated last evening by the 'Twelfth Night Revels.' It was replete with music and festival, and the population of the city turned out to see the procession." There were sixteen floats and with their reigning Lord of Misrule, the Revelers revealed not only their Anglo-Saxon leanings and love of the ancient English holiday, but they successfully blended it with the Creole love of Carnival.

At the ball there was "an immense Twelfth Night cake . . . upon the front of the stage. . . . Suddenly with his wand, the Harlequin struck the cake." The stage curtains then opened to disclose the Lord of Misrule seated on a throne next to Cleopatra. Presently pieces of the cake were distributed among the guests to choose a queen, but it was all a rather fumbling affair as court fools and jesters distributed the pieces of cake on spears and in the end the bean finder did not come forward. The *Times* complained that while there was a cake and pieces of it were distributed, "fancy, *if* you can, 'Twelfth Night' *without a bean!*" In 1871 the presentation of the cake slices was better arranged and monitored, and the Lord of Misrule was able to successfully crown a Twelfth Night queen.

The Twelfth Night Revelers paraded for only six seasons, but the organization still stages its ball, which is private. From its inception in 1870, organized Carnival in New Orleans was no longer just the Mistick Krewe of Comus on Mardi Gras night. The Carnival season now had a formal beginning, which truly melded the Christmas season with the Carnival season.

In the words of the *Times*, "Before this year [1870], the 'King's Day' was unrecognized in the calendar of festivities. Hereafter, our people will look for it." But for the most part the press did not report on Twelfth Night activities, except for coverage of the Twelfth Night Revelers, as in the 1800s, Twelfth Night was a night for private parties. However, in 1897 the *Daily Picayune* ran an article about how to throw a Twelfth Night party, illustrating the growing recognition of the holiday. "Once, [it was] a time of great popular festivity," said the *Picayune*, but the paper saw it was being "resuscitated and brought back into general notice." The *Picayune* referred to Twelfth Night as "Little Christmas," an Irish term, which showed that it was still closely associated with Christmas, rather than Carnival, its more modern New Orleans guise.

Guests were to be "bidden" to come to the party "before sunset," soon after which a great cake was to be served. The *Picayune* did not call it a king cake as New Orleanians do today, but referred to it by its old English name, a Twelfth Night cake. Whoever received the tokens—there were two—baked in the cake became the king and queen of the revels. At the time a silver dime was appropriate for the king, while a silver thimble was for the queen. Guests did not cut their own pieces of cake; they were cut and individually distributed by the host. The monarchs directed all the games and amusements of the party and each guest had to willingly play the "devoted subject." This was in the style of Twelfth Night parties of the Middle Ages, but all in good fun and respectable to fit the tastes and proprieties of the late nineteenth century.

The *Daily Picayune* gave its readers an "old recipe" for what it described as a "very large" Twelfth Night cake:

> Wash two cups of butter and beat it until it is creamy; add four cups of granulated sugar and the grated rind and juice of one lemon. Stir into this mixture the yolks of twelve eggs, putting in one at a time, and beating it well before adding the next one. Dissolve a teaspoonful of soda in two cups of milk and gradually stir into the other ingredients. Add three cups of sifted flour, and then part of the whites of the dozen eggs beaten to a stiff froth; add three more cups of flour with two teaspoonfuls of cream of tartar, and then the remaining eggs, and last two cups of flour. Flavor with wine or a little brandy. Put the cake mixture into

a large, round pan lined with buttered paper. Place the silver pieces on opposite sides of the cake, and stick a broom splint in the side of the cake to show which is for the men. . . . Put the pan containing the cake in a moderate oven and let the cake bake slowly at first, and cover the top with a paper, if it should brown too rapidly. When the cake is baked it should be covered with a thick white frosting, ornamented around the upper edge of the cake with a wreath formed of the frosting and candied violets, rose leaves and cherries and diamond-shaped leaves cut from thin slices of citron and stuck here and there.

While today's king cakes are decorated with icing and/or piles of loose sugar tinted in purple, green, and gold, this was not so in 1897 when, according to the *Picayune,* Twelfth Night decorations should reflect Christmas. On the middle of the cake the newspaper recommended that a toy Christmas tree about six inches high "such as can be bought at any toy store" be placed along with three figures to represent the three kings. One miniature king was to be placed where the broom splint (a long, thin strip of wood slivered off the wooden handle of a broom) was pulled out so that the server would be able to recognize which side of the cake should be handed out to the men.

Christmas decorations of green and scarlet were deemed most appropriate for the party. The paper suggested that a large horseshoe made of red carnations, representing good luck for the New Year, be hung from the chandelier over the table where the cake was served. The horseshoe was a replacement for the scarlet bell used on Christmas. It was also recommended that green vines trail down from the horseshoe onto the table. Considerable candlelight was also deemed ideal.

Christmas Meets Carnival

Although Twelfth Night is the official beginning of the Carnival season, Carnival events can transpire before January 6. Mardi Gras can occur as early as February 3, and in those years when Mardi Gras falls so early, some of the balls have to be held before Twelfth Night in order to fit into a tight schedule.

Rex, the King of Carnival, was founded in 1872, and soon after began issuing his proclamation in the city's newspapers the day after Christmas to remind everyone that Mardi Gras would soon arrive. Another loose connection Rex has with Christmas is his grand march. It is the Grand March from Giuseppe Verdi's opera *Aida,* which had its world premier in Cairo on Christmas Eve in 1871, just a few months before the first Rex parade.

Then there's Harlequins, which deliberately holds its annual ball during the Twelve Days of Christmas. This group, which began in 1925, holds a masquerade ball for youthful members of society, rather than for adults. The decorations in their ballroom reflect Christmastide. Even earlier in the Christmas season is the ball of the Squires, which takes place prior to Christmas Eve. Like Harlequins, Squires is composed of younger members of the community and has been active since 1964. During the Squires' tableau (a brief presentation during the ball) little boys enter the ball dressed as reindeer.

Phunny Phorty Phellows and the Revival of Twelfth Night

The most recent public incarnation of Twelfth Night revelry dates all the way back to 1878—but then only in name. On March 5, the date of Mardi Gras that year, the Phunny Phorty Phellows (PPP) was born and followed the Rex parade. Prior to the birth of the PPP there had been 1870s versions of ragtag second liners following Rex that were not welcomed by the king of Carnival. Rex embraced the more organized PPP with its fantastic theme, bizarre floats, political satire, and general irreverence. It was a complete surprise to the public and

On Twelfth Night the Phunny Phorty Phellows board the St. Charles Avenue streetcar and announce to one and all that Carnival has officially begun. (Photo by Jules Richard IV)

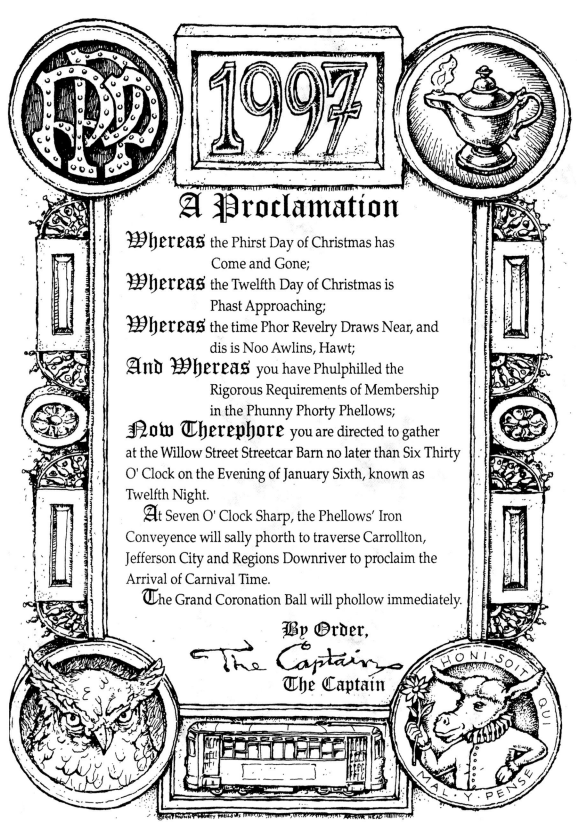

1997

A Proclamation

Whereas the Phirst Day of Christmas has
Come and Gone;

Whereas the Twelfth Day of Christmas is
Phast Approaching;

Whereas the time Phor Revelry Draws Near, and
dis is Noo Awlins, Hawt;

And Whereas you have Phulphilled the
Rigorous Requirements of Membership
in the Phunny Phorty Phellows;

Now Therephore you are directed to gather
at the Willow Street Streetcar Barn no later than Six Thirty
O' Clock on the Evening of January Sixth, known as
Twelfth Night.

At Seven O' Clock Sharp, the Phellows' Iron
Conveyence will sally phorth to traverse Carrollton,
Jefferson City and Regions Downriver to proclaim the
Arrival of Carnival Time.

The Grand Coronation Ball will phollow immediately.

By Order,
The Captain
The Captain

*For many years the revived Phunny Phorty Phellows have announced their historic
Twelfth Night streetcar ride in the form of a proclamation. This one was designed by
New Orleans artist Arthur Nead. (Courtesy of Peggy Scott Laborde)*

The Phunny Phorty Phellows are always masked and costumed on the annual ride.
(Photo by Harriet Cross)

an instant sensation. The PPP symbol was an owl, and their motto was "A little nonsense now and then is relished by the best of men." They continued to follow Rex for eight years, until 1885, coming to be called the "dessert of Carnival." After 1885, the Phunny Phorty Phellows stopped parading but continued to hold a ball. They resumed parading from 1896 to 1898 before disbanding altogether.

Although the krewe went out of existence, the long saga of the PPP does not end there. In 1981 their illustrious name was resurrected by a group of Mardi Gras enthusiasts. The new Phunny Phorty Phellows first paraded as part of the Krewe of Clones, which was the impetus to today's highly irreverent Krewe du Vieux. The Phunny Phorty Phellows, whose hallmarks are humor and whimsy, differ from their predecessors in that they no longer parade on or just before Mardi Gras but since 1982 have proclaimed the start of the Carnival season by a streetcar ride on Twelfth Night.

Before the masked and costumed riders board the streetcars

This masked member of the Phunny Phorty Phellows lifts his glass to toast the beginning of the Carnival season. (Photo by Peggy Scott Laborde)

New Orleans photographer George Long got the baby in his slice of king cake during the ride of the Phunny Phorty Phellows. He became the Boss (the Phellows' king) in 2007. (Photo by Harriet Cross)

Phellows must wear a mask and costume during their streetcar ride. (Photo by Peggy Scott Laborde)

The Storyville Stompers provide the music during the annual Twelfth Night streetcar ride of the Phunny Phorty Phellows. (Photo by Peggy Scott Laborde)

for their journey that includes stretches of St. Charles Avenue and Canal Street, there is a Carnival countdown. During the ride and to the accompaniment of the Storyville Stompers, the Boss (the PPP's traditional name for their king) and queen are chosen in the traditional manner by election through king cake. Invitations and dance cards are in the style of the late nineteenth century. After their streetcar ride, the group moves on to a coronation ball at Mid-City Lanes Rock 'n' Bowl. Their musical entertainment? The quintessentially New Orleans band Benny Grunch and the Bunch.

If Twelfth Night originally signaled the end of Christmas, in New Orleans it now ushers in the Carnival season, and the Phunny Phorty Phellows are the official herald. When they cut a ribbon in front of their streetcar announcing, "It's Carnival Time" prior to boarding, the magic of Christmas has stepped aside for another year to let the revelry of Carnival rule.

In Perry Young's seminal work on the New Orleans Carnival, *The Mistick Krewe: Chronicles of Comus and His Kin*, he writes, "Carnival is a butterfly of winter whose last real flight of Mardi Gras forever ends his glory. Another season is the season of another butterfly, and the tattered, scattered, fragments of rainbow wings are in turn the record of the day."

And right before that butterfly comes along each year with its rainbow wings how fortunate we are to be able to celebrate Christmas in New Orleans. At this time of the year, with City Park's ancient oaks covered in moss and decorations, who knows, maybe a cocoon is nestled in one of those majestic branches.

The authors would like to acknowledge the generous assistance of The Historic New Orleans Collection in providing many of the images contained in this book.

THE COLLECTION
THE HISTORIC NEW ORLEANS COLLECTION
533 Royal Street • 70130-2179 • www.hnoc.org • (504) 523-4662

The Historic New Orleans Collection is a privately endowed museum and research center located in the heart of the French Quarter. It was established in 1966 by Gen. and Mrs. L. Kemper Williams, avid collectors of materials related to Louisiana history and culture.

Located inside a complex of historic buildings at 533 Royal Street are the Williams Gallery, where changing exhibitions are available to the public at no charge; ten permanent exhibition galleries devoted to illustrating the history of the city, state, and Gulf South, where docent-guided tours are available at a modest fee; the historic residence of General and Mrs. Williams, where guided tours are also available; and a museum shop. This is one of the most significant groups of buildings in New Orleans and includes the house built by Jean François Merieult, where The Collection's main entrance is located on Royal Street. Dating from 1792, the Merieult House survived the great fire of 1794, making it one of the oldest structures in New Orleans. Other buildings on the property date from the nineteenth century, including the Williams residence, built in 1889.

The Williams Research Center, at 410 Chartres Street, is located in a former police station and jail built in 1915. Following an extensive renovation by The Collection, it was opened to the public in 1996. The Collection's research facilities originally were located in three separate reading rooms at the Royal Street complex, serving the library, manuscripts, and pictorial divisions. The Williams Research Center allowed the reading rooms to merge as one beautifully designed facility, thus providing greater availability of materials and convenience to both patrons and staff. The Williams Research Center is open free of charge to anyone interested in studying New Orleans and Louisiana, and while shelves are closed to browsers, staff is able to assist with The Collection's extensive holdings of manuscripts, books, and images.

A more recent addition to The Historic New Orleans Collection is an entirely new building adjoining the Williams Research Center. Opened in 2007, it is designed with a public meeting space on the ground floor and three floors of state-of-the-art vaults above. The façade of the new building, which fronts on Conti Street, replicates the appearance of a nineteenth-century hotel that once stood on the site. The Collection has also acquired several neighboring French Quarter buildings, including the famed Brulatour Courtyard across Royal Street from The Collection's original Royal Street complex.

Bibliography

Anderson, Brett. "Reveillon Revelry: Holiday Dinners Rebound at Restaurants This Season." *The Times-Picayune,* Lagniappe, 9 December 2005.

Armstrong, David. "A Creole Christmas: In New Orleans, There's No Revel Like Reveillon." *San Francisco Chronicle,* Travel, 10 December 2000.

Bowler, Gerry. *The World Encyclopedia of Christmas.* Toronto, Canada: McClelland & Stewart Ltd., 2000.

Bremer, Fredrika. *The Homes of the New World: Impressions of America.* Translated by Mary Howitt. 1853. Reprint, New York: Negro Universities Press, 1968.

Capote, Truman. *One Christmas.* New York: Random House, 1983.

"Celtic Mythology and Celtic Religion." Heart o' Scotland. Available from http://www.heartoscotland.com/Categories/CelticMythology.htm.

"Christmas Lights." Wikipedia: The Free Encyclopedia. Available from http://en.wikipedia.org/wiki/Christmas_lights.

"Classic! A Celebration of Sugar Bowl Memories, Presented in Recognition of the Donation of the Sugar Bowl Archive to The Historic New Orleans Collection." The Historic New Orleans Collection, November 29, 2007-January 13, 2008. Exhibition Catalogue.

Collins, Ace. *Stories Behind the Best-Loved Songs of Christmas.* Grand Rapids, MI: Zondervan, 2001.

Cooper, Virginia M. *The Creole Kitchen Cook Book.* San Antonio: The Naylor Company, 1941.

Cranow, Gus. "Fires on the Levee." *New Orleans Magazine,* December 1980.

Dabney, Thomas Ewing. *Historic Holmes: The Growth of a Great Business Institution and a Great City.* New Orleans: D. H. Holmes Co., 1925.

"Deep in Dixie: New Orleans' First Christmas." *The Times-Picayune New Orleans States Magazine.* December 21, 1947.

Elliott, Jock. *Inventing Christmas: How Our Holiday Came to Be.* New York: Harry N. Abrams, Inc., 2002.

Forbes, Bruce David. *Christmas: A Candid History.* Berkeley: University of California Press, 2007.

Forsythe, Michael. "Christmas in New Orleans." *New Orleans Magazine,* December 1987.

Frost, Meigs O. "New Orleans' First Christmas 216 Years Ago." *Times-Picayune Magazine,* December 23, 1934.

Gaudet, Marcia G. *Tales from the Levee.* Lafayette, La.: Center for Louisiana Studies, University of Southwestern Louisiana, 1984.

Gravois, Carol. "Bonfires on the Levee: A Family Tradition in Ascension Parish." Folklife in Louisiana, the Louisiana Folklife Program, Louisiana Folklore Society. Originally published in *Louisiana Folklore Miscellany,* 1991.

Available from http://www.louisianafolklife.org/LT/Articles_Essays/
main_misc_bonfires_levee.html.

Guidry, Emily Chenet. "Bonfires on the Levee." St. James Parish.com. Available
from http://www.stjamesparish.com/local/localinfo/BONFIRES/bonfir1.
htm.

Hardy, Lady Helen. "Le Grand Diner Creole, Le Jour De l'An 1850." *New
Orleans Magazine*, December 1969.

Hearn, Lafcadio. *Lafcadio Hearn's Creole Cook Book*. 1885. Reprint, Gretna, La.:
Pelican Publishing Company, 1990.

Hendrickson, Robert. *The Grand Emporiums: The Illustrated History of America's
Great Department Stores*. New York: Stein and Day, 1979.

Huber, Leonard V. *Creole Collage*. Lafayette, La.: Center for Louisiana Studies,
University of Southwestern Louisiana, 1980.

Huber, Leonard V., and Samuel Wilson, Jr. *The Basilica on Jackson Square: The
History of the St. Louis Cathedral and Its Predecessor 1827-1987*. New Orleans:
St. Louis Cathedral, 1987.

Jumonville, Florence M. "With the Compliments of the Season." *The Historic
New Orleans Collection Quarterly*, Winter 1990.

Kane, Harnett T. *The Southern Christmas Book*. New York: David McKay
Company, Inc., 1958.

Kirk, Susan Lauxman, and Helen Michel Smith. *The Architecture of St. Charles
Avenue*. Gretna, La.: Pelican Publishing Company, 1977.

Laborde, Errol. "O Holy Light: A Christmas Tour of Stained Glass Windows."
New Orleans Magazine, December 1989.

Laborde, Peggy Scott. "Christmas in New Orleans." WYES-TV, Greater New
Orleans Educational Television Foundation, 2006.

Laborde, Peggy Scott, and John Magill. *Canal Street: New Orleans' Great Wide
Way*. Gretna, La.: Pelican Publishing Company, 2006.

LaCour, Arthur Burton, and Stuart Omar Landry. *New Orleans Masquerade*.
New Orleans: Pelican Publishing Company, 1952.

Laussat, Pierre Clément de. *Memoirs of My Life*. Translated by Sr. Agnes-
Josephine Pastwa. Baton Rouge: Louisiana State University Press for The
Historic New Orleans Collection, 1978.

Leach, William. *Land of Dreams: Merchants, Power, and the Rise of a New American
Culture*. New York: Pantheon, 1993.

"Mad Orleans Yuletide of 1803 Holds Eating Record." *Times-Picayune*, 19
December 1937, sec. 2, p. 5.

Magill, John. "Canal Street Is 150 Years Old." *New Orleans Preservation in
Print*, December 1985.

——. "Canal Street's Glamorous History." *New Orleans Preservation in Print*,
December 1988.

——. "Street Smarts: Canal a History." *New Orleans Magazine*, June 1998.

Magill, John, Mary Lou Eichhorn, and Mark Cave. "In a New Light." *Louisiana
Cultural Vistas*, Winter 1999-2000.

McNulty, Ian. "Reveillon Dinners: Awakening the Holiday Spirit One Feast at
a Time." New Orleans French Quarter.Com. Available from http://www.
frenchquarter.com/dining/reveillon.php.

The Original Picayune Creole Cook Book. 9th ed. New Orleans: The Times-
Picayune Publishing Company, 1938.

"A Brief History of the Phunny Phorty Phellows." The Phunny Phorty Phellows.
Available from http://www.phunnyphortyphellows.com/history/.

The Picayune's Creole Cook Book. 2nd ed. New Orleans: The Picayune, 1901.

Points, Marie Louise. "Clopin-Clopant: A Christmas Fragment of Early
Creole Days." *The Daily Picayune*, 25 December 1892.

Ripley, Eliza. *Social Life in Old New Orleans: Being Recollections of My Girlhood.* 1912. Reprint, New York: Arno Press, 1975.

Roach, John. "Christmas Eve Bonfires Light Up Louisiana Levees." *National Geographic News*, 21 December 2006. Available from http://news.nationalgeographic.com/news/2006/12/061221-new-orleans.html.

Robin, C. C. *Voyage to Louisiana, 1803-1805.* Translated by Stuart O. Landry, Jr. New Orleans: Pelican Publishing Company, 1966.

Rowland, Dunbar, ed. *Official Letter Books of W. C. C. Claiborne 1801-1816.* Jackson, Miss.: State Department of Archives and History, 1917.

Russo, Mary T. "Carriers' Addresses." In *A Checklist of American Newspaper Carriers' Addresses, 1720-1820.* Worcester, Mass.: American Antiquarian Society, 2000. Available from http://dl.lib.brown.edu/carriers/essay_intro.html.

"Samhain: The Celtic Roots of Hallowe'en." Fravahr.org. Available from http://www.fravahr.org/spip.php?article407.

Schindler, Henri. *Mardi Gras: New Orleans.* Paris: Flammarion, 1997.

Smith, Rebecca. "Classic! A Celebration of Sugar Bowl Memories." *The Historic New Orleans Collection Quarterly,* Fall 2007, 2-5.

Transit Rider's Digest in "Cruise Cards: Holidays/Christmas" at the Williams Research Center, The Historic New Orleans Collection. December 23, 1963; December 30, 1968; December 27, 1971; December 15, 1972; and December 20, 1982.

Transit Rider's Digest in "Cruise Cards: Weather" at the Williams Research Center, The Historic New Orleans Collection. February 10, 1958; February 9, 1959; January 16, 1961; February 19, 1968 and September 14, 1981.

Trosclair, Carroll. "Christmas Eve Bonfires." Suite101.com. Available from http://louisiana-travel.suite101.com/article.cfm/christmas_eve_bonfires.

Newspapers

L'Abeille de La Nouvelle-Orléans
Frank Leslie's Illustrated Newspaper
Harper's Weekly
The Illustrated London News
New Orleans Daily Picayune
New Orleans Daily True Delta
New Orleans Item
New Orleans States
New Orleans States-Item
New Orleans Times
New Orleans Times-Democrat
New Orleans Times-Picayune

Index